A Taste of the West Country

A collection of original recipes created by
Taste of the West award-winning chefs and producers

wemakemagazines

A catalogue record for this book is available
from the British Library.

ISBN 978-0-9933352-3-5

Published by We Make Magazines Ltd
wemakemagazines.co.uk

Editor: Jennie Cooper
Sub-editor: Raphael Chapell
Designer: Jeff Cooper

Thanks to Jo Hall, Julie Hutchins and Jody Spencer.

Meat

Lamb chops, tomato fondue, crushed
new potatoes and salsa verde   34

Roast rack of lamb, broccoli purée,
cheese dumplings and Potatoes Anna   36

Picanha steaks, blue cheese butter and triple-cooked chips   40

Pan-fried ribeye steak with mustard
pomme purée and Bourguignon sauce   42

Christmas turkey salad   46

Turkey ballotine, roast potatoes and tenderstem broccoli   48

Rustic salami winter stew   52

Asparagus with poached duck egg, hollandaise and salami   54

Hog's Pudding Scotch eggs   58

Sausage skewers with a honey and balsamic glaze   60

BBQ glazed ribs with hash browns and fried eggs   62

Goat's cheese and rosemary cheesecake with a
coppa crisp, honeycomb and hazelnut garnish   72

Steak, Stilton and Lyonnaise onion toasted sarnie   80

Ribs with cider and maple glaze   92

Duck breast with blackcurrant vodka and plum sauce   104

Jerk chicken wings with pineapple salsa   116

Fish

Mussels in ale   88

Cod with asparagus, crushed new potatoes, samphire,
red spring onions, and a white wine and chive sauce   98

Grilled oysters with sparkling white wine cream sauce   100

Mackerel fillets marinated in rapeseed oil   110

Pollock in lime & ginger sauce,
Mexican salad and habanero mayonnaise   114

Vegetarian

Cremet, chestnut mushroom and seasonal greens risotto 66

Goat's cheese mousse with spiced plums,
rocket, hazelnuts and water biscuits 70

Smoked cheddar Dauphinoise potato
gratin with crispy crumb topping 74

Sourdough bread 78

Smashed avocado, poached egg and
chipotle chilli on toasted sourdough 82

White onion, cheddar and ale soup 86

Desserts

'Cheese board' and ice cream dessert,
with pears and walnut praline   68

Raspberry cider and thyme sabayon,
with grilled peaches and apricots   94

Rapeseed oil cake, with buttermilk and rosemary ice cream   108

Doughnut fritters with orange curd and chocolate ice cream   120

Coffee ice cream and banana sundae with salted liqueur sauce   122

Lemon posset with ice cream,
summer fruits and mini meringues   124

Clotted cream fudge brownie, ice cream and summer berries   128

Vanilla clotted cream fudge and chocolate babka buns   130

Salted Caramel & Pecan Fudge iced
parfait with candied pecans   134

Chocolate and peppermint fudge   136

Foreword

The West Country is renowned for its food scene, and every year sees hundreds of entries into the Taste of the West Awards.

Our rich pastures and clear waters are an ideal landscape for growing and farming in, but it's the combination of this, alongside the talent of dedicated growers, producers, farmers and chefs, that make the winning combination. We have plenty to be proud of, which is why we produce this ever-popular recipe book.

Now in its fourth year, *A Taste of the West Country* has, once again, paired award-winning chefs and producers from the Taste of the West Awards to create this locally-inspired keepsake. Each pair comes from Cornwall, Devon, Dorset and Somerset, bringing you special recipes, using the finest local produce.

Using ingredients readily available across the region, these dishes are created uniquely for this book — straight from the chef's kitchen! You needn't be an accomplished cook to recreate them at home — all have been compiled using easy-to-follow steps, with some handy chef's tips to help you along the way.

Not only will you impress your friends and family with these dishes, but you are also supporting our local food and drink industry. What better way to celebrate a true Taste of the West Country? We hope you enjoy cooking (and eating) our recipes.

John Sheaves
Chief Executive, Taste of the West

All recipes serve 4

Our West Country

Meet the people behind the food

The recipes in this book are designed to be prepared at home, but we encourage you to visit the award-winning pubs, restaurants and hotels featured to enjoy similar dishes prepared by the pros.

The producers' locations are also indicated with a page number where you can read their full story. If the producer sells online – which most in this book do – the website address will be on its page.

Darren Beare, Cornish
Pantry, Cornwall Gold

CORNWALL

● Deli Farm Charcuterie
(Page 50)

Brian Etherington
Meat Company
(Page 56) ●

● Treway Farm Turkeys
(Page 44)

● **The Rising Sun**

● **Cornish Pantry**

● **Mullion Cove Hotel**

With its award-winning chefs, The Cornish Pantry has an imaginative menu using delicious Cornish produce, all sourced within 20 miles. From a full Cornish breakfast served on a miner's shovel, to its famous pasty platter, there is something to suit all tastes.

Gold winner in the Casual Dining category.
cornwall-gold.com

Experience award-winning Cornish cuisine, bursting with flavour at the Mullion Cove Hotel. From Helford River Oysters to the finest Cornish fish, prime steak to excellent vegan dishes, it takes no shortcuts in bringing you the freshest and best of the season.

Gold winner in the Restaurant category.
mullion-cove.co.uk

The Rising Sun offers superb food, showcasing local, seasonal produce.
Tom Hannon, a hands-on owner and dedicated chef, is incredibly knowledgeable about seasonable produce and regularly changes his menu to make the most of the quality ingredients that Cornwall has to offer.

Gold winner in the Dining Pub category.
risingsuntruro.co.uk

Paul Stephens, Head Chef, Mullion Cove Hotel and
Mark Etherington, Brian Etherington Meat Company.

Will and Kate Martin, Treway Farm Turkeys

Katie Hannon, The Rising Sun; Martin Edwards, Deli Farm Charcuterie; Thomas Hannon, Head Chef/Proprietor, The Rising Sun; Jean Edwards, Deli Farm Charcuterie

Steve Williams, Owner and Marcus Davey, Head Chef, The Pig & Pallet

The Vanilla Pod ●

"You will be welcomed as a guest, and leave as a friend" say Dasha and Ronnie Moughton, owners of the Vanilla Pod in Lynton, North Devon. Enjoy English, Mediterranean and Middle Eastern delights. Dasha recommends the mezze, "Three dishes can be shared as a starter for two people, or make a perfectly varied main course for one."

Gold winner in the Café / Tearoom category.
thevanillapodlynton.co.uk

DEVON

The Pig & Pallet is a quirky, vibrant restaurant with a relaxed atmosphere, making it a great place for a night out with friends. Local sourcing is a high priority and the dishes have maximum flavour.

Gold winner in the Casual Dining category.
pigandpallet.co.uk

Roly's Fudge (Page 126) ●

Orange Elephant ●
(Page 118)

● **The Pig & Pallet**

● LWC South West (Page 90)

Sea Trout Inn ●
Waterside Bistro ●　● Hallett's the Bakers (Page 76)
● Sharpham (Pages 64 & 96)

The Sea Trout, a family-run 15th-century coaching inn, ticks all the boxes for an authentic country pub. The Stags Bar has low beams and a roaring fire, 11 luxury en-suite bedrooms and a beautiful beer garden complete the picture.

Gold winner in the Dining Pub category.
theseatroutinn.co.uk

Waterside Bistro on The Plains in Totnes, has an enviable reputation for good food at a great price. Seafood is a speciality.

The restaurant is owned and run by Matt and Delphine Buzzo. Matt strives to build relationships with local suppliers to find the best Devon has to offer.

Silver winner in the Casual Dining category.
watersidebistro.com

Dasha and Ronnie Moughton, The Vanilla Pod Restaurant

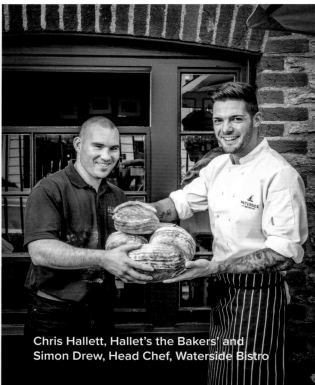
Chris Hallett, Hallet's the Bakers' and Simon Drew, Head Chef, Waterside Bistro

Simon and Lauren Newhouse, Owners, Sea Trout Inn

Matt Pugh and Matt Jones, Roly's Fudge

Duncan Schwab, Head Winemaker, Sharpham
and Matt Buzzo, Chef/Proprietor, Waterside Bistro

The Somerset Hotsauce Company ●
(Page 112)

Best Western Plus Centurion Hotel ●

Fussels Fine Foods (Page 106) ●

Godminster (Page 102) ●

● **Castle Bow Restaurant**

● Coombe Farm Organic (Pages 32 & 38)

● **The Lordleaze Hotel**

SOMERSET

Castle Bow Restaurant offers a fine dining experience in a relaxed setting. Bread is baked in the Castle's kitchen, chutneys and jams are made using apples from the Castle's orchard, and herbs come from the Norman garden.

Gold winner in the Restaurant category.
castlebow.com

The privately-owned Best Western Plus Centurion provides a professional service, in a warm environment. The award-winning restaurant's à la carte menu showcases the freshest seasonal produce, featuring elegant and imaginative dishes.

Gold winner in the Restaurant category.
centurionhotel.co.uk

The Lordleaze Hotel, once an 18th-century farmhouse, is a comfortable country hotel, offering the finest standards, with a warm and friendly atmosphere.

Gold winner in the Restaurant category.
lordleazehotel.com

George Cornwall & Dominic Vincent, Coombe Farm Organic,
Liam Finnegan, Executive Head Chef, Castle Bow Restaurant

Sean Horwood, Head Chef, Best Western Plus Centurion Hotel with Doug Pennock and Lewis Clark, Directors, The Somerset Hotsauce Company

Richard Hollingbery, Founder/Managing Director, Godminster

Tom Holloway, Head Chef, Alexandra Hotel and Ben White, Coombe Farm Organic

Matt Street, Executive Chef, Seasons Restaurant at the Eastbury Hotel, (centre), Tim Fussell and Lizzy Etheridge, Fussels Fine Foods

Jim Jones, Tenanted Trade Director, Palmers Brewery

Darren Batten, Head Brewer/Director, Palmers Brewery, Jaap and Hannah Schep, The Three Horseshoes

The Eastbury Hotel

Alexandra Hotel & Restaurant ●

● Palmers Brewery (Page 84)

The Three Horseshoes

DORSET

Dog friendly, children welcome, muddy boots allowed! "Our aim is to be a pub where we would be happy to spend our free time," say owners Jaap and Hannah Schep. The menus reflect the local area, and change regularly to ensure the seasonality of the produce.

Gold winner in the Dining Pub category.
threehorseshoesburtonbradstock.co.uk

The Alexandra is a boutique hotel set within private gardens overlooking Lyme Bay, Cobb Harbour and across the Jurassic Coast. Wake up to the perfect view.

Gold winner in the Restaurant category.
hotelalexandra.co.uk

The Eastbury Hotel offers a range of dining and drinking spaces, each with their own individual character and atmosphere. Enjoy the Hotel's award-winning Seasons Restaurant or dine on the alfresco Terrace.

Gold winner in the Restaurant category.
theeastburyhotel.co.uk

LAMB

What makes the best cut of lamb? George Cornwall
and Dominic Vincent, from Coombe Farm Organic
in Crewkerne, Somerset, give their verdict

Each part of a lamb is delicious in its own right, but if you are talking about the 'king of cuts', anything from the loin is out of this world. It's tender texture and flavoursome fat makes for a perfect combination, and it doesn't take long to cook either.

A rack of lamb is very special. The time and effort put in to trimming and chining the bones, and the spectacle it is when cooked, makes you fall in love with food, not only for the flavour but also for the theatre too!

Cooking cuts of meat on the bone gives maximum flavour. This enhances the complex flavours the muscle itself has developed from the many months our flock grazes on lusciously rich mixed grasses (organic, of course, and slow-grown). This is how sheep would have been farmed many generations ago. All of which results in award-winning meat!

Coombe Farm Organic is a Gold and Silver winner in the Meat & Poultry category.

Visit the website to buy online:
coombefarmorganic.co.uk

Lamb chops, tomato fondue, crushed new potatoes and salsa verde

Recipe by Sean Horwood, Best Western Plus
Centurion Hotel, Bath, Somerset

Ingredients

4 Barnsley lamb chops from Coombe
 Farm Organic
8 Jersey Royal potatoes
8 black olives, finely chopped

For the tomato fondue

800g chopped tomatoes
1 clove of garlic, crushed
1 red onion, finely diced
½ bunch coriander, roughly chopped
25g sugar
25ml red wine vinegar
2 tbsp capers

For the salsa verde

Few sprigs each of mint, parsley and
 basil
1 clove of garlic, peeled and chopped
2 tbsp capers
2 anchovies, finely sliced
1 heaped tbsp Dijon mustard
100ml extra virgin olive oil
2 tbsp red wine vinegar
Sea salt and pepper

Method

To make the tomato fondue

1 Drop a drizzle of olive oil into a saucepan, add the onions and garlic, and sweat down slowly. Drain the chopped tomatoes, add to the pan and bring to a simmer for five minutes, then add the sugar and vinegar.
2 Slowly reduce the mixture down, and keep stirring occasionally until thick and shiny.
3 Leave to cool slightly, then add the capers and coriander and keep aside until needed.

To cook the chops, potatoes and salsa verde

1 Preheat the oven to 180°C/gas mark 4.
2 Put the potatoes on to boil in salted water until softened, then drain and scrape them. Leave in a pan to keep warm.
3 Combine all the salsa verde ingredients until a paste consistency is reached — either in a pestle and mortar, or a food processor.
4 Heat an ovenproof pan on the stove, add a drizzle of olive oil and pan-fry both sides of the lamb chops until browned, then season with salt and pepper.
5 Transfer to the oven in the pan for six minutes for a pink centre. Remove and leave to rest in the pan.
6 Pour the pan juices into the potatoes, add the chopped olives and crush with a potato masher.
7 Serve on a plate with a spoonful each of the tomato fondue and crushed potatoes, then drizzle over the salsa verde.

Baby carrots or asparagus are a nice accompaniment to this dish.

Roast rack of lamb, broccoli purée, cheese dumplings and Potatoes Anna

Recipe by Liam Finnegan, Executive Head Chef,
Castle Bow Restaurant, Taunton, Somerset

Ingredients

2 racks of lamb from Coombe Farm
    Organic (French trimmed)
1 clove of garlic
1 sprig of fresh rosemary
2 broccoli heads
100ml single cream
6 potatoes
200g goat's cheese, such as
    Sharpham Ticklemore
250g butter
1 egg, beaten
A handful of breadcrumbs
100g plain flour
Olive oil
A glass of red wine
125ml vegetable or chicken stock
Salt and pepper

Method

For the dumplings

1 Remove the cheese rind, blend in a food processor, and roll into 30g balls.
2 Roll the cheese balls in flour, wash with egg, then roll in breadcrumbs. Chill.

For the broccoli purée

1 Separate the green florets from the stalk and set the latter aside.
2 Finely chop the florets, blanch in rapidly boiling water for three minutes, drain and set aside.
3 Trim and thinly slice a quarter of the stalk and set aside for serving. Chop and cook the remaining stalk in a separate pan with the cream, salt and pepper.
4 Once cooked through, add the blanched broccoli to the cooked stalk mixture, blend in a food processor, then pass through a chinois or sieve.

For the Potatoes Anna

1 Thinly slice the potatoes and layer them in a baking tray, brushing lightly with butter, and seasoning each layer with salt and pepper.
2 Bake at 140°C/gas mark 1 for 60 minutes.
3 Once cooked, serve immediately or place in the fridge to portion later.

For the lamb rack

1 Preheat the oven to 180°C/gas mark 4.
2 To fully render the meat's fat, lightly score it, then place it fat-side down in a hot pan.
3 Cook slowly and once golden all over, add some lightly crushed garlic and rosemary.
4 Place on an oven tray, then oven-cook for ten minutes. Remove and allow to rest on a rack for ten minutes.
5 De-glaze the lamb pan with a glass of red wine and some stock, heat, and reduce the jus by half.

To serve

1 Warm the broccoli purée and stalks in a saucepan, season with salt and olive oil.
2 Cut the potato into portions and either warm in a pan with the sauce, or place in the oven when cooking the lamb.

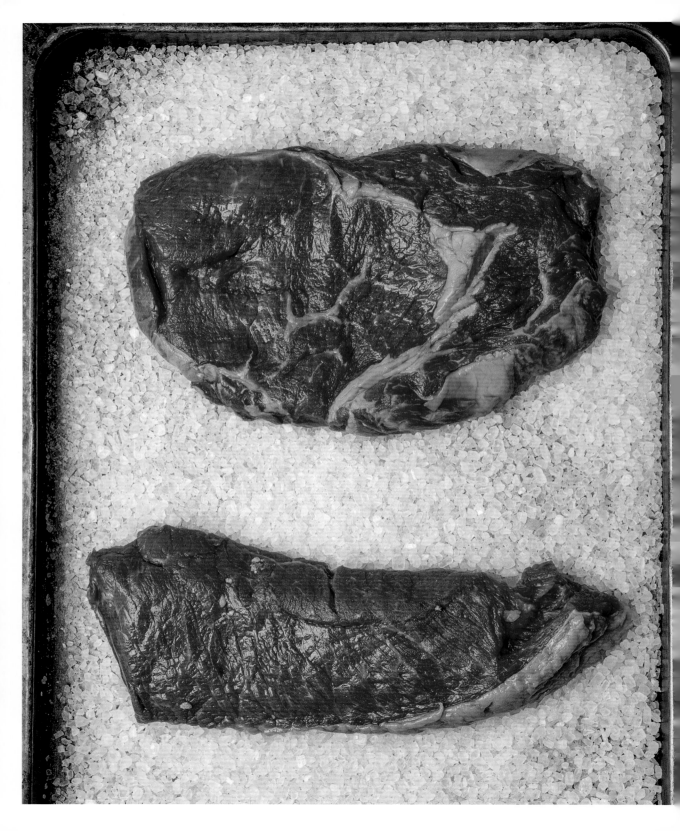

BEEF

What does it take to produce award-winning beef? Ben White, General Manager from Coombe Farm Organic in Crewkerne, Somerset, tells us

We are so lucky to farm here. The valley produces beautifully rich grass, which makes growing cattle to create succulent beef a symbiotic relationship with our terroir. We take care of the land, and it takes care of us by producing award-winning beef.

Here at Coombe Farm Organic, we believe in minimum waste — from how we farm, to the packaging we use, and even down to the style of butchery we have embraced. 'Seam' butchery is where we take each muscle from an animal and make the best use of it dependent on its structure, size and fat content.

This is how we came about cutting our beloved picanha steak. The rump of a beef animal is essentially made up of three muscles. Usually, a butcher would cut across all three and create a rump steak comprising a little of each, but we like to separate the tail, eye and cap — from which we cut picanha steaks. They eat much like a sirloin, but without the price tag.

Few know about the picanha so it isn't exactly a family staple, unlike the better-known rump or sirloin steak. But we love it so much that we continue to cut them, despite being a little more difficult to sell than a traditional three-muscled rump steak.

Coombe Farm Organic's Ribeye Steak was awarded Gold, and its Organic Picanha Steaks, Highly Commended in the Meat & Poultry category.

Buy online at: **coombefarmorganic.co.uk**

Picanha steaks, blue cheese butter and triple-cooked chips

Recipe by Tom Holloway, Head Chef, Alexandra Hotel, Lyme Regis, Dorset

Ingredients

Picanha steaks from Coombe Farm
    Organic
150g salted butter, softened
50g of blue cheese, such as Dorset
    Blue Vinney
8 large Maris Piper potatoes
Salt and pepper

Method

1 To make the chips, peel and wash the potatoes then square them off with a knife. Cut each potato into lengths about the thickness of your thumb. Boil in a pan of salted water until tender, but not falling apart. Drain.

2 Heat a deep fat fryer to 150°C/gas mark 2 and cook the chips for about six minutes, drain on some kitchen paper and leave to cool. Turn the fryer up to 180°C/gas mark 4.

3 Chop up the cheese, add to the softened butter and mix well.

4 Season the steaks with salt and pepper, then heat a frying pan to hot. Add a little oil, then gently place the steaks into the pan, turning every couple of minutes. Cook for about six to seven minutes for a medium-rare steak, then leave to rest for a further six to seven minutes.

5 While the steaks are resting, put the chips back into the fryer and cook until golden and crisp. Add a knob of the blue cheese butter to the top of the steaks and serve with a small dressed salad.

Pan-fried ribeye steak with mustard pomme purée and Bourguignon sauce

Recipe by Joe Nagy, Head Chef, The Lordleaze Hotel, Chard, Somerset

Ingredients

4 x 8oz ribeye steaks from Coombe
    Farm Organic
1 tbsp olive oil
100g pancetta, or smoked streaky
    bacon, diced
350g shallots
250g chestnut mushrooms (about 20)
2 cloves of garlic, sliced
1 tbsp tomato purée
500ml rich red wine (Burgundy is
    good)
Thyme sprigs
2 bay leaves

For the mustard pomme purée

6 medium potatoes, peeled and
    roughly chopped
50g butter, chopped
80ml cream
Salt and cracked black pepper
2 tbsp wholegrain mustard

Method

1 Heat a deep frying pan and add the olive oil. Season the beef and fry until golden brown, for about three to five minutes on each side, adding more oil if necessary. Leave to one side to rest.
2 In the same pan, fry the bacon, shallots, mushrooms and garlic until lightly browned. Mix in the tomato purée and cook for a few more minutes, stirring it well into the mixture, to enrich the Bourguignon.
3 Pour over the wine, add the thyme and bay leaves and bring to the boil for three to five minutes. Use a spoon to scrape the caramelised cooking juices from the bottom of the pan (this will give more flavour).
4 Boil the potatoes in a large saucepan for 20 minutes, or until soft. Then drain and return to the pan.
5 Add the butter, cream, salt and pepper, and mash until smooth and combined.
6 Transfer the mash to a large serving bowl and add the mustard.

To serve

Spoon a serving of the pomme purée on to a plate, and top with a steak and some sauce.

TURKEY

Will and Kate Martin's family-run Treway Farm Turkeys, near Grampound in Cornwall, is a successful enterprise with an emphasis on animal welfare

Treway Farm Turkeys is a family business, run by husband and wife team Will and Kate Martin, son Charlie, daughter Flora and Labrador Reuben. With its 300 acres of rolling hills and deep valleys just outside Grampound in Cornwall, Treway Farm is a perfect place to rear free-range bronze Cornish turkeys, alongside a commercial Limousin beef herd and Pedigree Shorthorn cattle.

Will says: "We took ownership of Treway in 2007 and have built up a herd of 200 Limousin cross cattle. We started producing our bronze turkeys back in 2010 for a few friends and family, and have slowly developed into the business we are today. This year, we will be rearing 800 birds for Christmas!"

Will continues: "Treway Farm Turkeys was the first Cornish producer to be accredited with the Golden Turkey Standard — an assurance scheme which guarantees the highest welfare standards for the birds, and stipulates that they must be reared using traditional methods and fed a natural diet. This gives them exemplary flavour. The turkeys spend their time roaming our meadows by day and are kept safe in their barn by night. In December, our turkeys are expertly dry hand-plucked and game-hung, which allows the meat to develop its full well-rounded flavour."

"We love producing the centrepiece of everybody's most special meal of the year. Although it does rather mean that we spend our own Christmas Day feeling absolutely shattered," Kate adds.

Treway Farm Turkeys is a Gold winner in the Meat & Poultry category.

Order your Free-Range Bronze Christmas Turkey online at: **trewayfarmturkeys.co.uk**

45

Christmas turkey salad

Recipe by Paul Stephens, Head Chef, Mullion Cove Hotel, Mullion, Cornwall

Ingredients

2 free-range Bronze Christmas Turkey Legs from Treway Farm Turkeys (roasted, skin removed and kept aside, leg meat shredded)
100g rocket
1 mozzarella ball
80g dried cranberries
3 slices Serrano ham
100ml cranberry juice
½ tsp Dijon mustard
100ml olive pomace oil
Salt and pepper

Method

1 Preheat the oven to 180°C/gas mark 4. Place the Serrano ham and turkey skin in between two sheets of baking paper and two metal trays. Cook until crispy (about 25 minutes) and leave to cool.
2 To make the dressing, reduce the cranberry juice to a syrup and add the Dijon mustard. Using a hand blender, slowly add the olive oil. If it starts to get too thick, add a little warm water to loosen.
3 Divide the rocket between four plates. Rip the mozzarella roughly, season, then add to the salad. Add the cranberries and the shredded turkey meat. Then break the crispy ham and turkey skin into shards and place on top of the salad.
4 Finish with the cranberry dressing.

Turkey ballotine, roast potatoes and tenderstem broccoli

Recipe by Paul Stephens, Head Chef, Mullion Cove Hotel, Mullion, Cornwall

Ingredients

1 Bronze Christmas Turkey Breast from Treway Farm Turkeys (butterflied and tenderised, see tip)
300g sausage meat
65g dried cranberries, roughly chopped
8 slices of Serrano ham
4 non-waxy potatoes
1 bunch tenderstem broccoli
1 onion, chopped
1 star anise
300g red wine
300g chicken stock
A glug of olive pomace oil for roasting
Salt and pepper

Chef's Tip:

Your butcher can do this for you, but if you'd like to have a go, make a vertical incision down the middle of the breast and cut both ways, not quite to the edge. It should fold open like a book, at which point, cover with baking paper and lightly tenderise.

Method

To make the ballotine

1 Arrange three layers of cling film, roughly the size of a piece of A3 paper. Wipe flat with a tea towel.
2 Place the eight slices of Serrano ham in two rows, slightly overlapping each other – this should leave you with plenty of excess cling film.
3 Place the flattened turkey breast slightly off-centre on the ham. Season with salt and pepper.
4 Mix the sausage meat and cranberries, and place in the centre of the breast.
5 Using the excess cling film as leverage, roll the ham and turkey around the sausage meat. Once sealed, keep rolling until the breast squashes up like a big pig-in-blanket, then tie the cling film at each end.
6 Heat a large pan of water to 80°C and keep it on a low flame to maintain this temperature.
7 Put a plate upside down on the bottom of the pan, then place the turkey parcel on top. During cooking, keep checking the water level and temperature.
8 After four hours the turkey will be cooked, so remove it from the water and allow to rest.

To make the sauce and cook the potatoes

1 Preheat the oven to 200°C/gas mark 6.
2 Caramelise the onion with the star anise and add the red wine, reducing the liquid by half. Add the chicken stock and reduce this further on a high heat, until the sauce coats the back of a spoon.
3 Peel and cut the potatoes, then boil in salted water for five minutes until the edges start to rough up. Remove from the water and allow to dry.
4 Heat some oil in a tray, add the potatoes, season with salt and pepper, and roast at around 200°C/gas mark 6 for 40 minutes, or until golden brown.

To make the finished dish

1 Heat a heavy-bottomed pan with a little oil. Carefully unwrap the ballotine and colour it in the pan, turning often to get an even colour. Slice each end off, then cut into four equal portions.
2 Steam or boil the broccoli for a few minutes until tender. Serve with the potatoes and drizzle with the red wine sauce.

CURED MEAT

Jean & Martin Edwards from Deli Farm Charcuterie in Delabole, Cornwall, stress the importance of a product's quality, which has led them to many awards

Deli Farm Charcuterie was one of the pioneering British producers to preserve meat by air drying, launching its then small range of salami at the end of February 2006. Its range and output has steadily increased, but maintains the quality of handcrafted artisan products.

The Garlic and Hot Peppery Salami are traditional flavours; its recipes have been carefully developed by Jean and Martin. Both flavours were in some of the very first salami that Deli Farm Charcuterie produced. However, last year they tweaked the recipes slightly and now, both are among its best sellers.

Using a combination of quality local pork, freshly ground herbs and spices, modern technology and time, this commitment to quality has been rewarded each year by achieving Taste of the West Awards since they started. "Entering the Awards is very important for us and our products. It shows that we have attained a standard that is recognised by consumers and wholesalers," says Jean.

With a commitment to sourcing local meat with low food miles, and using 100% renewable energy, Deli Farm can genuinely claim that its products are made with a minimal carbon footprint!

Deli Farm Charcuterie was awarded Silver for its Rustic Garlic Salami and Rustic Hot Peppery Salami in the Cured Meat category.

Available at delicatessens and farm shops throughout the country and direct from the company's online shop.

delifarmcharcuterie.co.uk

Rustic salami winter stew

Recipe by Darren Beare, Head Chef, Cornish Pantry, Redruth, Cornwall

Ingredients

400g Hot Peppery Salami (sliced) from Deli Farm Charcuterie
400g cannellini beans
150ml good red wine
12 shallots, peeled
400g chopped tomatoes
4 leeks, chopped
4 cloves of garlic, crushed
Olive oil
200ml chicken stock
180g red rice
12 piccolo tomatoes, halved
125g parmesan cheese, grated
Salt and pepper

Method

1 Boil the rice for 30 minutes, drain, then rinse under cold water and set aside.
2 In a pan, heat a little oil and fry the shallots for about four minutes, then add the leeks and garlic, and cook for a further two minutes.
3 Add the red wine and reduce by half, then add the chicken stock and reduce by half again.
4 Pour in the chopped tomatoes and bring to a simmer. Add the cannellini beans, rice, salami and piccolo tomatoes, simmer for a further five minutes, then season.
5 Divide into four bowls, sprinkle with parmesan cheese.

Serve with warm bread.

Asparagus with poached duck egg, hollandaise and salami

Recipe by Thomas Hannon, Head Chef/Proprietor,
The Rising Sun, Truro, Cornwall

Ingredients

500g Cornish asparagus, stalks
  trimmed
4 free-range duck eggs
250g salted butter
2 egg yolks
Splash of white wine
Splash of white wine vinegar
120g Garlic Salami from Deli Farm
  Charcuterie (finely sliced into strips)
½ lemon, squeeze of juice
Salt and pepper

Method

To make the hollandaise sauce

1 Gently melt the butter in a pan over a low heat.
2 Once melted, slowly pour off the fats (the clarified/clear layer) and discard the butter milk.
3 Add the white wine, white wine vinegar and a pinch of salt to the egg yolks. Place in a bain-marie and whisk until it reaches soft ribbon stage (just holds its shape).
4 Take off the bain-marie and slowly pour in the clarified butter, whisking continually (it's handy to have another person to hold the bowl steady at this stage). The mixture should start to thicken.
5 Once all the butter is added, add a squeeze of lemon juice, and season to taste.

To make the poached eggs

1 Bring a pan of water to simmer and add a splash of white wine vinegar (this helps the eggs to hold their shape).
2 Using a wooden spoon, stir the water to create a whirlpool, then crack each duck egg into the centre. For soft poached eggs, cook for three to four minutes; for firmer eggs, four to five minutes.
3 Remove with a slotted spoon and drain.

For the rest of the dish

1 Pan-fry the salami strips, until golden brown and slightly crispy.
2 Blanch the asparagus in boiling water for two minutes, drain, and toss in a little butter.

To serve

Place the asparagus spears (all facing in the same direction) in the centre of a plate and then a duck egg on top. Pour a generous amount of the hollandaise over the egg and top with a sprinkle of Deli Farm's Garlic Salami.

Chef's Tip: If asparagus isn't in season, try with pak choi or purple sprouting broccoli.

SAUSAGES

Experience has led to growth for Mark Etherington,
Managing Director of the Brian Etherington Meat Company
in Scorrier, Cornwall

Our family business has been supplying the South West's hospitality sector with high-quality meats since 1954. We expanded in 2012 with a flagship Farm Shop at our base in Cornwall, which houses our artisan bakery, butchery academy and development kitchen, where our gold-awarded Hog's Pudding is created.

We've been making Hog's Pudding for over 50 years to the same traditional recipe, which includes quality pork, cereals, a range of herbs and chilli – and of course a few secret ingredients! Its slightly spicy nature and sausage-like texture means it's a must for breakfasts, great with seafood, or delicious on its own. We've also incorporated it in some of our other handmade products, including our Hog's Pudding Sausage Rolls, which are incredibly indulgent.

I am extremely proud of how our Hog's Pudding has developed – originally created in small batches in the butchery at my grandfather's house – to now being made in a £30,000 state-of-the-art catering kitchen.

This year, we are further expanding the business with an online butchery shop, selling our dry-aged Cornish Beef and other Taste of the West award-winning products: Baconberg, Cornish Pasties, Ribs in a BBQ sauce and of course, our Hog's Pudding.

Gold and Silver winner in the Sausage, Savoury Bakery and Meat & Poultry categories.

etherington-meats.co.uk

Hog's Pudding Scotch eggs

Recipe by Paul Stephens, Head Chef, Mullion Cove Hotel, Mullion, Cornwall

Serves 6

Ingredients

6 eggs
200g sausage meat
100g Hog's Pudding from Brian
   Etherington Meat Company
   (cooked and grated)
10 tbsp water
1 tsp chopped thyme leaves
20g French mustard
1 tsp cayenne pepper
4 tbsp chopped chives
Salt and pepper
Flour, whisked eggs and breadcrumbs
   (in bowls to coat the eggs)

For the dip

200g mayonnaise
50g English mustard

Method

1   Bring a pan of salted water to the boil. Carefully place the eggs into the water and cook for five minutes. Remove and place into iced water until cold.
2   Once the eggs have cooled, carefully peel off the shells.
3   Put the sausage meat and Hog's Pudding into a blender with the water, and pulse a few times until incorporated. Transfer to a bowl, then mix in the French mustard and other ingredients and season with salt and pepper.
4   Divide the mixture into 55g portion balls and place each one on to cling film. Use another piece of cling film to flatten the mixture, keeping it as circular as possible.
5   Remove the top layer of cling film and place an egg on the sausage meat. Using the remaining cling film, wrap the eggs in the meat, making sure they are fully covered. Leave to set in the fridge for 30 minutes.
6   Coat the Scotch eggs in flour, eggs, then breadcrumbs.
7   Deep fry them at 190°C/gas mark 5 for two minutes, then transfer into the oven, also heated to 190°C, for 10 minutes.
8   Mix the mayonnaise and English mustard together to serve as a dip for the Scotch egg.

Sausage skewers with a honey and balsamic glaze

Recipe from Etherington's Farm Shop, Scorrier, Cornwall

Ingredients

1 yellow bell pepper, chopped
1 red onion, chopped
12 vine-ripened cherry tomatoes, chopped
6 sprigs of rosemary
6 Wheal Rose Pork Sausages from the Brian Etherington Meat Company
2 tbsp balsamic vinegar
2 tbsp runny honey
1 clove of garlic, crushed
1 handful of sesame seeds
Salt and pepper

Method

1 Make the balsamic glaze by mixing the vinegar, honey, garlic and sesame seeds together into a bowl until combined.
2 Coat the pepper, onion and tomatoes in the glaze, season with salt and pepper.
3 Cut each sausage into thirds and thread, alternating with the vegetables, onto the rosemary sticks. If you're using regular kebab sticks, soak them in warm water for 15 minutes before adding to the heat.
4 Cook over a grill, or on the barbecue, for 10–12 minutes turning occasionally, until the sausages are cooked through and the vegetables are chargrilled.
5 Serve with couscous.

BBQ glazed ribs with hash browns and fried eggs

Recipe by Paul Stephens, Head Chef, Mullion Cove Hotel, Mullion, Cornwall

Ingredients

3 racks of cooked Wheal Rose Glazed
   Pork Ribs from Brian Etherington
   Meat Company
140g mashed potato
10g parsley leaves, finely chopped
4 eggs
1 egg yolk
1 punnet cherry tomatoes
10ml white wine vinegar
½ tsp Dijon mustard
100ml olive pomace oil
Watercress
Salt and pepper

Method

1 Place one rack of ribs in the microwave and heat on full power for 30 seconds. Remove from packet and wipe off the BBQ sauce with kitchen towel.
2 Take the meat off the bones and shred with a couple of forks. Mix with the mashed potato, chopped parsley and egg yolk.
3 Season with salt and pepper and shape into hash browns, then allow to set in the fridge for half an hour.
4 To make a tomato dressing using a liquidiser or hand blender, combine the cherry tomatoes, vinegar and mustard. With the blades still running, slowly incorporate the oil. If the dressing becomes too thick, add a little water to loosen. Season with salt to taste.
5 Heat the remaining racks either in a microwave or oven, and divide between four plates.
6 While they are heating, add a little oil to a heavy-bottomed pan. Once hot, fry the hash browns gently on each side for a couple of minutes. Remove from the pan and finish cooking in a medium oven for five minutes.
7 Use the same pan to fry the eggs in.

To serve

Drizzle with the tomato dressing and garnish with watercress.

CHEESE

Producing a quality product is all about the raw materials, according to Mark Sharman, Managing Director of Sharpham Wine and Cheese in Ashprington, Devon

Sharpham has been producing top quality, highly-acclaimed cheese and wine on the family farm at Sharpham Estate, in Ashprington near Totnes, for over 37 years.

Looking further back, its own herd of Jersey cows has been producing rich, tasty milk for 66 years!

Mark says: "Because we want to make exceptional cheeses, we take the provenance and quality of all our raw materials very seriously. We clearly have our own source of cow's milk, but in terms of goat's and sheep's milk, it means sourcing from farmers who understand milk is both a food and an ingredient, and not just a commodity product. These are people who understand we want the best, freshest, most natural milk we can get."

"Making cheese by hand in the laborious, traditional way is how we choose to do it, having deliberately not mechanised our processes. Handling milk and curds gently and with respect does pay dividends in the final product," Mark explains.

"Sharpham Cremet is one of our new cheeses developed by Head Cheesemaker Debbie Mumford, to combine the best of goat's milk and cow's cream, and Sharpham Savour is now established as an intriguing mix of cow's and goat's milk.

"The greatest satisfaction comes from watching people enjoy our artisan cheeses while taking a tour of the farm complete with wine and cheese tastings," he adds.

Gold, Silver and Highly Commended winner in the Cheese category.

Sharpham Cremet is the Taste of the West 2017: Cheese Champion Product and the Supreme Champion Product.

Buy online at: **sharpham.com**

Cremet, chestnut mushroom and seasonal greens risotto

Recipe by Thomas Hannon, Head Chef/Proprietor,
The Rising Sun, Truro, Cornwall

Ingredients

1 onion, finely diced
2 cloves of garlic, finely chopped
1 knob of salted butter
400g risotto rice
100ml white wine
1l warm vegetable stock
200g chestnut mushrooms
100g asparagus (diagonally chopped)
100g peas
100g rainbow chard
100g sugar snap peas
400g Sharpham Cremet from
    Sharpham Wine and Cheese
    (roughly chopped)
Bunch of chopped parsley to garnish
Salt and pepper

Method

1 Gently sweat the onions and garlic in a pan for three or four minutes (to soften, not to colour).
2 Add the risotto rice and stir for approximately two minutes.
3 Add the white wine.
4 Once the risotto rice has absorbed the white wine, start to add the stock, a ladleful at a time, continually stirring until all the stock has been absorbed (usually after around 20 minutes). Check the seasoning.
5 While cooking the risotto, lightly fry the chestnut mushrooms in a pan until golden brown. Drain and add to the risotto.
6 Blanch all the green vegetables in boiling water for 90 seconds, drain and add to the risotto.
7 Gently fold in the Cremet.
8 Finish with a handful of parsley. If the risotto is a little thick, loosen with a small amount of white wine or vegetable stock.

Chef's Tip: The vegetables can be easily adapted to suit preferences and growing seasons. Roasted beetroot is an unusual, yet delicious addition.

"This is a great dinner party dish and looks impressive served in a large pan in the middle of the table." Thomas Hannon

'Cheese board' and ice cream dessert, with pears and walnut praline

Recipe by Kris Jury, Head Chef, Sea Trout Inn, Staverton, Devon

Ingredients

For the ice cream
1l of double cream
120ml of rum
3 gelatine leaves
240g pasteurised egg
300g sugar
1 tsp lemon juice
100g blue cheese

For the pears
4 conference pears
500ml red wine
500ml water
100g sugar
Cinnamon stick
Cloves
1 vanilla pod

For the walnut praline
300g walnuts
300g sugar

4 slices each of Sharpham Rustic and
Sharpham Ticklemore Goat Cheese
from Sharpham Wine & Cheese

Method

To make the ice cream
1 Whisk together the egg, sugar and lemon juice.
2 Soak the gelatine leaves in cold water.
3 Warm the rum, then add the gelatine to the alcohol, trying not to allow too much water to get into it.
4 Combine the gelatine mixture with the eggs.
5 Whisk the cream into soft peaks, then carefully stir it into the gelatine mixture.
6 Add the crumbled blue cheese and freeze for 12 hours.

To prepare the pears
1 Peel the pears carefully and level their bases, to enable them to stand up.
2 Combine all the ingredients into a large pot and gently simmer.
3 Once the fruit is softened, but still holding its shape, remove and cool – be careful not to overcook it.

To make the praline
1 Heat the sugar in a pan over a high heat until just golden – be careful not to burn it.
2 Add the nuts and spread over a non-stick baking sheet to cool.
3 Once cooled, blitz in a food processor until a crumb-like consistency.

To serve
1 Place a spoonful of praline on the dish.
2 Stand a pear up on top of the praline.
3 Scoop a large ball of blue cheese ice cream next to the pear.
4 Add a slice each of the Sharpham cheeses, and drizzle the dish generously with the liquor from the pears.

Goat's cheese mousse with spiced plums, rocket, hazelnuts and water biscuits

Recipe by Liam Finnegan, Executive Head Chef,
Castle Bow Restaurant, Taunton, Somerset

Ingredients

400g goat's cheese (for best results use a crumbly, semi-set cheese)
120g thick natural yoghurt
30g fresh rocket leaves
6 plums
Rosemary Water Biscuits from Godminster
50g hazelnuts
100ml balsamic vinegar
300g olive oil
20g plain vegetable oil
A small pinch of each of these spices: cumin, star anise, Chinese five-spice and cayenne pepper
1 clove of garlic
5g of fresh ginger
Salt and pepper

Method

To make the cheese mousse

1 Remove the cheese rind and leave it to come up to room temperature.
2 Blend it in a food processor with the yoghurt until smooth, then season.
3 Place the mixture in a disposable piping bag and leave to rest in the fridge until serving.

To make the spiced plums

1 Quarter the plums and lightly chargrill. It's up to you how many pieces you wish to char – you can mix them with some uncooked plums too.
2 In a pan, warm 20g vegetable oil and add a small pinch of each of the spices, along with the garlic and ginger. Smell, taste and adjust the heat using the cayenne pepper.
3 Once the oil and spice blend is warmed, add the chopped plums, heat, then reduce to a simmer.
4 When the fruit is soft and cooked, remove the garlic and ginger and place them in a food processor.
5 Blend well, pass through a sieve and allow to cool.
6 Place the spiced plums in balsamic vinegar for 20 minutes.

To serve

1 Remove the plums from the balsamic vinegar and dress the plate.
2 Place the balsamic vinegar in a pan to heat, reducing by half to intensify.
3 Cut the bottom of the piping bag and pipe the mousse on to the plate.
4 Whisk the reduced balsamic vinegar with the garlic and ginger oil, and dress the hazelnuts and rocket leaves.
5 Serve with the Godminster Rosemary Water Biscuits and enjoy!

Chef's Tip: Leftover goat's cheese? Pipe it and roll into small balls, then flour, egg wash, roll in breadcrumbs and freeze. They are perfect for pre-dinner nibbles at your next party, or fried and served with salad.

Goat's cheese and rosemary cheesecake with a coppa crisp, honeycomb and hazelnut garnish

Recipe by Matt Street, Executive Chef, Seasons Restaurant at The Eastbury Hotel, Sherborne, Dorset

Ingredients

For the cheesecake base
25g toasted hazelnuts
200g Rosemary Water Biscuits from Godminster Farm
110g melted butter
A pinch of salt

For the cheesecake filling
250g goat's cheese
100g soft cream cheese
150ml double cream
1 sheet of bronze leaf gelatine
Sprig of rosemary

To garnish
Honeycomb pieces (or honey)
1–2 slices of air-dried/coppa ham
25g toasted hazelnuts, crushed

Method

To make the cheesecake base and the garnish
1   Toast all the hazelnuts (50g).
2   Take the air-dried ham and bake in the oven for ten minutes at 160°C/gas mark 3, or until crispy.
3   To make the base, blitz the butter, water biscuits, 25g of hazelnuts, plus a pinch of salt, in a food processor, until the mixture forms a cheesecake-base consistency.
4   Transfer this into a lined, six-inch square tray (cling film works best), pat the base flat and even, then put in the fridge to chill.

To make the cheesecake mix
1   Add the goat's cheese (warmed to room temperature) to the soft cheese.
2   Warm the cream, adding the sprig of rosemary.
3   Soften the gelatine leaf in cold water, remove the rosemary sprig from the cream and add the gelatine.
4   Combine both the cheese and cream mixtures together to form a smooth texture, pour on to the cake base, and chill in the fridge for four hours.

To serve, cut into portions and decorate with the garnish.

Smoked cheddar Dauphinoise potato gratin with a crispy crumb topping

Ingredients

750g floury potatoes (such as Maris Piper or King Edward)
284ml double cream
200ml full-fat milk
2 cloves of garlic, smashed
6 sprigs of thyme
Pinch of nutmeg
½ brown onion, peeled but kept whole
150g Oak-Smoked Cheddar, from Godminster Farm (grated)
100g Panko breadcrumbs
4 tbsp Parmesan cheese, grated
Butter for greasing
Salt and pepper

Method

1 Preheat the oven to 180°C/gas mark 4.
2 Peel and thinly slice the potatoes. Cook in plenty of lightly salted water for about five minutes. Drain and set aside.
3 Pour the cream, milk, garlic, three sprigs of thyme leaves, nutmeg and onion into a saucepan and bring to just before the boil. Remove from the heat, then strain through a fine sieve into a jug.
4 Grease a gratin dish with butter. Place a layer of the potatoes in the bottom, then season with salt and pepper, and sprinkle with a little of the smoked cheddar. Repeat the process, layering the potato, cheddar and seasoning until there are no remaining ingredients.
5 Pour the cream mixture over the top and allow it to soak in, pressing down lightly on the potatoes.
6 In a bowl, mix the breadcrumbs, remaining thyme leaves (stripped from their stalks and stalks discarded), Parmesan cheese and season. Sprinkle over the gratin and bake for about 45 minutes until golden and bubbling.

To serve

You could serve this with the duck breast recipe on page 104 and greens on the side, or on its own with greens or a salad.

BREAD

A long-established business, Hallett's the Bakers in Paignton, Devon, has captured a market with its award-winning Natural Sourdough and Multiseed Bread

Hallett's the Bakers was founded in 1993, on Winner Street in Paignton, by husband and wife team Mel and Helen Hallett. With four staff, the bakery and coffee shop had a turnover of £30,000 a year. Some 25 years later, with the help of the staff and the couple's sons Christopher and Luke, it now employs 30 people with an annual turnover of over £1.5 million.

"We have built our business steadily, always focused on providing a service and product that exceed expectations. We supply to both retail and restaurants who demand the best, locally baked goods." says Chris Hallett, Director and Bakery Manager.

"The bakery relies on a diverse customer base, and the need for repeat business is crucial to our success. This requires the highest levels of consideration, from taking an order in the afternoon, making fresh goods, wrapping and packing over night, then dispatching the next morning before sunrise. Our team is our business, and it's them that help us to keep moving forward."

Hallett's Natural Sourdough uses just three basic ingredients: flour, water and salt, plus a long fermentation process to increase its flavour. As Chris explains: "A slow prove develops the Sourdough's flavour profiles. It takes eight hours, which bakers think is a long time these days, but this bread requires it."

"Our Sourdough was something new we tried around two years ago. We saw a market for more traditional breads, so introduced it. This style of bread making is what customers are enjoying at the moment," adds Chris.

Here's to the next 25 years!

Gold and Silver winner in the Savoury Bakery category.

Available from retail outlets across South Devon, including the bakery's own shop in Paignton.

hallettsthebakers.co.uk

Sourdough bread

Recipe by Chris Hallett, Director and Bakery Manager, Hallett's the Bakers, Paignton, Devon

Ingredients
1kg strong white bread flour
700ml water
200g leaven (or yeast)
18g salt

Method
1 Mix the flour with 500ml of the water and all the leaven until it is combined.
2 Rest the dough for 30 minutes.
3 Mix in the remaining water and salt, and then knead the dough for 5 mins, or until smooth and slack.
4 Fold the outside of the dough into the middle on all four sides, then leave for 1 hour in a lightly oiled, covered container. A large margerine tub works well.
5 After 1 hour, fold again, rest for a further hour and fold once more.
6 Divide the dough into three equal pieces and 'round up'.
7 Cover it and rest for 15 minutes.
8 Mould into a round shape and place in a floured basket.
9 Leave the bread to rise (prove) for four hours at room temperature. For best results, chill for two hours before baking, to help give the dough its shape.
10 Preheat the oven to 245°C/gas mark 9.
11 Tip out of the basket onto a baking tray covered with parchment paper. Score with a sharp knife and steam bake for 35-45 minutes. If your oven doesn't have a steam setting, you could place a roasting tray with cold water in the bottom of the oven when you preheat it.

Optional: To make the leaven (plenty of time required!)
1 To make the leaven 'starter', mix 10g of white flour and 10ml of water into a plastic container with a lid, and keep warm for two to three days until bubbles form.
2 Refresh by adding 20g of starter, to 20g of flour and 20ml water and leave for two to three days.
3 Refresh again by adding 60g of the starter, to 60g of flour and 60ml water, to leave again for two to three days.
4 The starter needs to double in size overnight, this indicates the leaven is active and ready for bread making.
5 To refresh at this point, feed 100g of leaven with 100g of flour and 70ml of water. Once refreshed, leave the leaven for 24 hours, make some dough and repeat every day.
6 The leaven will last about a week refrigerated, but always feed 24hrs before use.

Steak, Stilton and Lyonnaise onion toasted sarnie

Ingredients

One sliced multi-seed loaf from
    Hallett's the Bakers
400g flank skirt steak, or bavette
100g Stilton cheese, sliced
2 brown onions, thinly sliced
Splash of olive oil, plus a dash for the
    steak
2–3 sprigs of thyme
1 fat clove of garlic, smashed
30g salted butter
50ml apple cider or white wine
    vinegar
50ml good quality beef stock
Salt and pepper

Method

1 Remove the beef from the fridge half an hour before cooking to allow it to come up to room temperature.
2 Meanwhile, to make the Lyonnaise onions, gently melt the butter in a heavy-based saucepan with a splash of oil. Throw in the onions, garlic and thyme sprigs and gently cook for five to ten minutes until softened.
3 Add the vinegar and cook down until almost reduced, then add the beef stock and reduce until the onions are soft and sticky. Taste, season to your liking, then set aside.
4 Heat a heavy-based skillet, or cast-iron pan, until smoking hot.
5 Rub some oil on the steak, season with salt and pepper, then carefully place the steak into the pan. Sear it on both sides for two to three minutes. Remove and allow to rest.
6 While the steak rests, toast the bread on both sides. Butter, then layer with the Lyonnaise onions and Stilton.

To serve

Cut the steaks into 1cm slices and add to the sarnie, top with the other slice of toasted bread and tuck in.

Smashed avocado, poached egg and chipotle chilli on toasted sourdough

Recipe by Matt Buzzo, Chef/Proprietor, Waterside Bistro, Totnes, Devon

Ingredients
1 Natural Sourdough loaf from Hallett's the Bakers
2 ripe avocados
4 free-range eggs
Juice of 1 lime
Salt and cracked black pepper
Chipotle chilli flakes

Method
1 Slice the sourdough as thick as you like and toast.
2 Open and scoop out the avocados into a bowl. Add the lime juice, salt and pepper and bash up with a fork until you have a texture that you can pile onto your toast.
3 Poach the eggs and place on top, with a generous sprinkle of chipotle.

Chef's Tip: For perfect poaching, crack the egg into an espresso cup. Then lower it gently into a pan of boiling water containing a capful of white wine vinegar.

BEER

Palmers of Bridport in Dorset has been brewing cask-conditioned ales since 1794 and continues to be successful

Palmers has been brewing authentic cask-conditioned real ales in the West Dorset market town of Bridport since 1794. "We have never felt the need to describe our ales as 'craft' because they have never been anything else," says Darren Batten Head Brewer and Director.

"This year we were delighted that two of our ales could feature in the Taste of the West recipe book. Tally Ho! is a deep, distinctive dark ale with delicious characteristics of fruit cake and roasted malt. It's our most awarded ale.

"Dorset Gold is a bright, upbeat golden ale, packed with zesty and thirst-quenching flavours. With strong links to the Jurassic Coast, its sales have supported coastal charities and organisations, most significantly the Chesil Trust, which has benefited from over £30,000.

"It is fantastic that one of our longest standing and most recognisable ales can feature here, alongside one of our fastest-growing brands," Darren concludes.

Silver and Highly Commended winner in the Beer category.

Palmers' bottled ales can be bought from the brewery's online shop: palmerswinestore.com

palmersbrewery.com

White onion, cheddar and ale soup

Recipe by Jaap Schep, Head Chef/Proprietor,
The Three Horseshoes, Burton Bradstock, Dorset

Ingredients

120g unsalted butter
700g large white onions
6 sprigs of thyme
400ml chicken stock
450ml Dorset Gold Ale from Palmers
200g crème fraîche
200g cheddar, grated
1 tsp sugar
Salt and pepper

Method

1 Place a large pan onto a medium heat and add the butter.
2 Once melted, add the onions, thyme and sugar.
3 Cook over a medium heat, stirring occasionally, until the onions are lightly caramelised and golden. This will take about 10–15 minutes.
4 Add the ale and chicken stock, bring to a simmer and cook for another 10 minutes.
5 Remove the pan from the heat, and stir in the cheddar and crème fraîche.
6 Remove the thyme stalks, pour the soup into a blender, and blend until smooth. Season to taste.

Serve with your favourite bread.

Mussels in ale

Recipe by Kris Jury, Head Chef, Sea Trout Inn, Staverton, Devon

**Serves 4 as a starter
or 2 as a main meal**

Ingredients
1kg of Exmouth mussels
1 bottle of Tally Ho! ale from Palmers
2 shallots
3 cloves of garlic
500ml pouring cream
Fresh parsley and chives, chopped
Rustic bread of your choice

Method
1　Rinse the mussels in cool, clean water and remove any beards.
2　In a heavy-based frying pan, sauté the chopped shallots and garlic. Once softened, add the mussels, ale and cream.
3　Place a tight-fitting lid on the pan and let the mussels steam until they have all opened.
4　After approximately seven minutes, remove the lid from the pan to see if all the shells have opened, discarding any that haven't.

Serve immediately with some sliced rustic bread.

CIDER

Duncan Bryan, Brands Development Manager at South West Orchards in Somerset, talks about this collaborative business

A stone's throw from the River Tone in Somerset, South West Orchards' Modern Craft Ciders are created using a blend of the finest West Country cider apples.

To achieve the perfect balance of crisp, sweet and bitter — we use local produce. Yarlington Mill, Harry's Master and Dabinett apples are blended with a small amount of dessert apple, to give the cider a delicious, fruity bite. To match Somerset's relaxed surroundings, the cider is fermented under ambient conditions, and then allowed to mature naturally, for at least three months. This ensures it is full of flavour, with a light sparkling touch.

South West Orchards is a collaboration between two renowned independent companies, both at the forefront of producing and distributing quality drinks: LWC Signature Brands and Sheppy's Cider.

LWC Drinks is the UK's largest independent distributor of beers, wines, spirits and soft drinks. Delivering quality products, the Signature Brands portfolio features carefully crafted creations, as well as handpicked imports.

Sheppy's Cider is an independent family cider-making business, owned and run by David and Louisa Sheppy. The family has been making the highest quality traditional Somerset ciders for 200 years, and continues to produce fine, traditional, bottled and draught ciders, as well as a range of sparkling and special interest ciders.

Gold winner in the Cider category.

southwestorchards.co.uk

Ribs with cider and maple glaze

Recipe by Marcus Davey, Head Chef, Pig & Pallett, Topsham, Devon

Ingredients

4 racks of baby back or belly ribs (ask the butcher to trim)

For the Pig & Pallet rib rub

100g salt
100g sugar
30g smoked paprika
20g onion powder
15g ground fennel
15g ground coriander
15g ground black pepper
15g garlic powder
5g chipotle powder
5g ground juniper
5g mustard powder

For the rib emulsion

1l Modern Craft Cider from South West Orchards
125g salted butter

For the cider and maple glaze

2l Modern Craft Cider from South West Orchards
500ml maple syrup
5 tbsp demerara sugar
BBQ sauce

Method

1. Combine all the rib rub ingredients well.
2. Rub the ribs with the mix and set aside for 30 minutes, but overnight if possible.
3. Heat the rib emulsion ingredients slowly in a pan to melt the butter. Using a stick hand blender, blitz and season.
4. BBQ the ribs slowly over an indirect heat at 110°C–120°C (lowest gas mark setting) for four hours.
5. Make a tin foil pouch and line this with greaseproof paper, which stops the ribs from sticking to the foil.
6. Place the ribs into the pouch, splitting the emulsion evenly between them. Close the pouch up, allowing a bit of air space so they can steam cook.
7. Cook in the BBQ or oven at 100°C–125°C (lowest gas mark setting) for two to four more hours, depending on the bite you want.

To make the glaze

1. Reduce the cider in a pan by half, add in the maple syrup and sugar, and simmer, reducing the liquid until the glaze thickens.
2. Once reduced, add an equal quantity of BBQ sauce and set aside to cool.

To serve

Place the ribs on a baking tray or BBQ rack, brush on the glaze, and warm for around 10 minutes in the oven before serving.

Raspberry cider and thyme sabayon, with grilled peaches and apricots

Recipe from Dasha Moughton, Head Chef,
The Vanilla Pod, Lynton, Devon

Ingredients

For the sabayon
3 egg yolks
95g granulated sugar
Few sprigs of thyme (leaving some for the garnish)
285ml Raspberry Cider from South West Orchards

For the fruit
2 peaches (unripe)
4 apricots (unripe)
Pistachio crumbs
Icing sugar

Method

To make the sabayon
1 Place all the ingredients (except the thyme) into a large bowl, set over a pan of simmering water.
2 Whisk until a thick ribbon forms – this can take a bit of time, so be patient, and don't stop whisking!
3 Once thickened, add the thyme leaves and give it a thorough final whisk. Pass through a sieve into a clean bowl, cool over ice, then set aside until required.

To prepare the fruit
1 Preheat the grill to very hot.
2 Cut the peaches and apricots in half, removing the stones.
3 Sprinkle the fruit halves with icing sugar, and place under the grill for five to seven minutes, or until the fruit starts to caramelise on top and soften slightly.

To assemble the dish
1 Place the cooled sabayon into four heatproof dishes and put under a very hot grill for a few minutes, until the top starts to caramelise.
2 Remove from the heat, and add half a peach and two apricot halves on to each dish.
3 Serve with some thyme leaves and pistachio crumbs. Enjoy with a glass of iced Raspberry Craft Cider from South West Orchards.

WINE

Duncan Schwab, Head Winemaker at Sharpham Vineyard in Ashprington, Devon tells us about the joy of winemaking

Sharpham Wine & Cheese has been part of the Sharpham Estate since 1981 – growing vines and farming the land – with a focus on producing a range of outstanding wine and cheese.

Over the past 15 years, Sharpham Vineyard has become a well-established favourite among locals and holidaymakers. We offer a diverse selection of options, from lunching in the lively alfresco Cellar Door café, to touring the vineyard, and tasting the hand-produced wine and cheese. Despite a consistent swell in the number of visitors, we have challenged ourselves to retain a personal, passionate and happy approach to welcoming everyone. Sharing what we do is part of the joy of doing it.

Many of our team members have been here for over 20 years, holding between them enough knowledge and wisdom to fill our biggest winemaking tank countless times over! It's a shared love of food, drink and the local area coupled with the ability to enjoy a good laugh that keeps us united through thick and thin.

When compared with other wineries globally, ours is very small. This means that the focus is on creating unique, exciting wines to bring out the best in a particular harvest or grape variety.

I have been making wine at Sharpham since 1992. I'm continuously inquisitive and open to results from different approaches and methods of transforming grapes into wine. There is no secret recipe to follow. We take each vintage on its merits and adapt our blends and winemaking to bring out the best characteristics of the year, and of course to make the best wines possible!

Gold, Silver and Highly Commended winner in the Wines, Spirits & Liqueurs category.

Sharpham Barrel Fermented 2014 is the Taste of the West 2017: Wines, Spirits & Liqueurs Champion Product.

Wine can be purchased from the vineyard and its website: **sharpham.com**

Cod with asparagus, crushed new potatoes, samphire, red spring onions, and a white wine and chive sauce

Recipe by Darren Beare, Head Chef, Cornish Pantry, Redruth, Cornwall

Ingredients

4 cod fillets (approx 220g)
16 new potatoes
4 red spring onions, halved
16 asparagus spears, trimmed
60g samphire
Small bunch of chives, chopped
150ml Dart Valley Reserve from
    Sharpham Vineyard
100ml fish stock
100ml double cream
75g unsalted butter
Salt and pepper

Method

1 Place the new potatoes in a pan of cold water with a little salt and bring to a simmer for 10–12 minutes.
2 Season the cod and heat a frying pan with a little butter and a little oil.
3 Place the spring onions and the cod skin-side down in the pan and cook for five minutes. Turn over and cook for a further five minutes.
4 Remove from the pan, drain the potatoes, and place the cod, potatoes and spring onions in a dish in the bottom of a low oven to keep warm.
5 Using the same pan, add the white wine and reduce by half, then add the fish stock and reduce by half again.
6 Add the cream and simmer until it coats the back of a spoon.
7 In another pan, fry the asparagus until tender, adding the samphire at the last minute.
8 Remove the sauce from the stove, add the chives, whisk in the remaining butter and season with salt and pepper.
9 Crush the new potatoes and place them on a plate with the asparagus, samphire, then the cod, spoon over the sauce and top with the onions.

Grilled oysters with sparkling white wine cream sauce

Recipe by Matt Buzzo, Chef/Proprietor,
Waterside Bistro, Totnes, Devon

Ingredients

24 rock oysters
A knob of butter
1 medium shallot, finely chopped
250ml Sharpham Sparkling Blanc
    wine from Sharpham Vineyard
1 bay leaf
250ml double cream
Salt and pepper to taste
100g hard cheese (such as Devon
    Oak), finely grated
A handful of breadcrumbs

Method

1 Open the oysters, turn them over in their bottom shell by cutting under the adductor muscle that holds them in. Keep the juice that will come from them.
2 In a saucepan, sweat the shallots in the butter until softened but without colouring them.
3 Add in the wine, bay leaf and reserved oyster juices.
4 Allow the liquid to reduce down until hardly any remains, before adding in the double cream.
5 Return to the boil, taste, then season to your liking.
6 Remove from the heat before dropping in the oysters.
7 Allow them to warm through for a minute, then place each one back in its shell with an equal amount of sauce. Sprinkle over the cheese and breadcrumbs.
8 Place under a hot grill, or very hot oven until the tops are deliciously brown and crispy.
9 Serve with the rest of the bottle of Sharpham, or if you've been having a sneaky taste, open another!

Santé!

Chef's Tip: Use scrunched up tin foil on a baking sheet to hold the oyster shells upright before filling with sauce and grilling. Serve straight from the foil.

VODKA

Provenance and flavour are key ingredients in Somerset-based Godminster Farm's award-winning Blackcurrant Vodka Spirit

Godminster Farm is set on the outskirts of the picturesque town of Bruton. With 1,300 acres of beautiful landscape, the farm is home to 280 organic dairy cows and has orchards filled with a variety of delicious fruits and herbs, which inspire many Godminster products. The award-winning Blackcurrant Vodka Spirit is rye-based, infused using fruit from the farm, with a rich aroma that delivers bursts of sweetness to the palate. With sustainability at the forefront of its beliefs, the team uses any fallen fruit from trees to minimise waste.

Managing Director and founder of Godminster, Richard Hollingbery, says: "We're best known for our delicious Vintage Organic Cheddar and we also create a range of artisan food to complement the cheese, inspired by the flavours around the farm. We believe that provenance is important when sourcing ingredients and it is key for us to choose the very best."

godminster.com

Duck breast with blackcurrant vodka and plum sauce

Served with smoked cheddar Dauphinoise potato gratin with crispy crumb topping (see page 74)

Ingredients

1 large banana shallot, finely diced
250g plums, stoned and roughly chopped
50g demerara sugar
1 star anise
150ml Blackcurrant Vodka Spirit from Godminster Farm
200ml good quality beef stock
4 duck breasts
Chinese five-spice
Knob of butter
Olive oil
Salt and pepper

Method

1 Preheat the oven to 180°C/gas mark 4. Heat a non-stick frying pan with a little oil, and fry the shallot for five minutes until soft but not coloured.

2 Add the plums and sugar, and shake around in the pan. Once the sugar has dissolved, add the star anise, vodka and stock.

3 Simmer for 15 minutes, stirring occasionally until the mixture reduces a little and thickens. Turn off the heat once it's at the right consistency, and set aside, removing the star anise.

4 While the sauce is reducing, drizzle the duck breasts with a little olive oil, then rub with the Chinese five-spice.

5 Heat a non-stick pan until hot. Place the duck breasts skin-side down and fry for six to seven minutes until they are a golden colour and the skin is crisp.

6 Turn them over and cook for two to three minutes on the other side. Add a knob of butter to the pan and, once it foams, baste the duck.

7 Transfer the duck to the oven and cook for five to six minutes for pink, or 10–12 minutes for well done.

8 Remove from the oven and allow to rest before serving with the sauce.

OIL

We find out a little behind the success of the award-winning rapeseed oil from Somerset-based Fussels Fine Foods

Tim Fussell, Sales and Production Manager at Fussels Fine Foods in Rode, Somerset, says: "We grow oilseed rape as a break crop within our four-year cropping rotation, and supply various farm shops and food services throughout the South and South West, together with national listings in supermarkets and online. A highlight of my job is seeing our product on the shelves, especially when I'm somewhere I didn't know stocks it."

Lizzy Etheridge, Production, Sales, Events and Hospitality at Fussels Fine Foods says: "I love the buzz of the Farmer's Markets and Shows, and interacting with customers. I loved the opportunity to drive our combine harvester and tractor with the seed drill. Over the course of a year, I have watched the crops with new eyes – from season-to-season, planting to harvest – with fascination and just a little knowledge. I feel a real connection with the land, the beauty of a newly drilled field, nurtured and eventually harvested, neatly baled, to finally seeing the rapeseed we've grown ready for pressing, bottling and selling to our customers."

Fussels Single Cold Pressed Extra Virgin Rapeseed Oil and Fussels Smoked Single Cold Pressed Extra Virgin Rapeseed Oil both won Gold in the Sauces & Accompaniments category.

For a list of stockists and to buy online, visit **fusselsfinefoods.co.uk**

Rapeseed oil cake, with buttermilk and rosemary ice cream

Recipe by Matt Street, Executive Chef, Seasons Restaurant at The Eastbury Hotel, Sherborne, Dorset

Ingredients

For the cake
180ml Extra Virgin Rapeseed Oil from Fussels Fine Foods
3 medium eggs
310ml milk
360g caster sugar
300g plain flour
1 tsp baking powder
1 tsp bicarbonate of soda
1 tsp salt

For the ice cream
600ml double cream
200ml milk
800ml buttermilk
300g caster sugar
12 egg yolks
100g rosemary
A pinch of salt

Method

1 To start the ice cream, place the cream, milk and buttermilk in a pan and warm to 80°C. Then, remove from the heat, add the rosemary, cover and allow to infuse for four hours.
2 Preheat the oven to 160°C/gas mark 3.
3 To make the cake, combine all the dry ingredients with the milk, oil and eggs until smooth.
4 Line a square, or eight-inch round cake tin with parchment paper, pour the cake mixture into the tin, making sure the batter is room temperature.
5 Bake at 160°C/gas mark 3 for 30–35 minutes or until golden brown.
6 Cool on a wire rack.
7 To make the ice cream, add the cream and milk mix to the egg yolks and sugar, and heat over a bain-marie until the mixture becomes a custard-like texture.
8 Remove from the heat and cool over ice – stir to prevent a skin forming.
9 Churn in an ice cream machine if available, or pour into a freezer-safe container and place into the freezer, mixing every 30 minutes or so for four hours to avoid ice crystals forming.
10 To serve, slice a portion of the cake, warm through, add a drizzle more oil, plus a drizzle of honey if you wish, and serve with the ice cream.

Mackerel fillets marinated in rapeseed oil

Recipe by Jaap Schep, Head Chef/Proprietor, The Three Horseshoes, Burton Bradstock, Dorset

Ingredients

50ml Smoked Rapeseed Oil from
    Fussels Fine Foods
4 large mackerel fillets, pin-boned
2 large beetroots, roasted and peeled
100g crème fraîche
100g watercress
20g fresh horseradish, grated
2 lemons
Salt and pepper

Method

1 Score the mackerel fillets and marinate in the oil for about four hours, saving a little oil for the rest of the dish.
2 Cut the beetroot into chunky wedges, place in a large mixing bowl, dress with some of the oil and lemon juice, and mix well. Season with salt and pepper.
3 Place a non-stick frying pan onto a medium heat, add a drizzle of the oil, then place the mackerel skin-side down in the pan.
4 Cook for about one minute on each side, depending on the size of the fillets.
5 Add the watercress to the beetroot and spoon on to the middle of the plate, and dress with crème fraîche.
6 Place the mackerel fillets on top of the salad and grate a little fresh horseradish over the dish.

SAUCES

Doug Pennock and Lewis Clark, founders of The Somerset Hotsauce Company in Bath, spotted a gap in the market – with huge success!

The Somerset Hotsauce Company is a small chilli sauce producer based in Bath. The company was founded in 2015 by two friends, Doug Pennock and Lewis Clark, to produce and sell a hot sauce recipe that Doug had created in 2013, and subsequently refined. The inspiration to start the company came when other local chilli producers began to comment on the uniqueness of the hot sauces, so Doug and Lewis saw a potential gap in the market that they could fill.

The chilli accompaniments are inspired by American Louisiana-style sauces and Asian spice infusions. "Combining chilli mashes with fresh ingredients, and a blend of freshly crushed herbs and spices, has created a range suitable for every heat-tolerance and with a focus on putting the flavours first," says Doug, adding: "The sauces are designed to be as versatile as possible, working well as dips, dressings, marinades and cooking ingredients."

In 2017, the company entered its current range of sauces (Original, Lime & Ginger, Pineapple and Habanero) into the Taste of the West Awards, winning three Golds and a Highly Commended.

Gold and Highly Commended winner in the Sauces & Accompaniments category.

somersethotsauce.co.uk

Pollock in lime & ginger sauce, Mexican salad and habanero mayonnaise

Recipe by Sean Horwood, Head Chef,
Best Western Plus Centurion Hotel, Bath, Somerset

Ingredients

400g pollock fillet
4 tbsp Lime & Ginger sauce from The Somerset Hotsauce Company
3 tbsp Habanero sauce from The Somerset Hotsauce Company
4 tbsp mayonnaise
½ white cabbage, finely sliced
100ml red wine vinegar
Olive oil
25g sugar
1 red onion, finely sliced (or use a mandolin)
6 breakfast radishes, finely sliced
1 bunch coriander, leaves chopped (stalks not needed)
1 avocado, chopped
Tin of black beans
4 corn tortillas
Salt and pepper

Method

1. Rub the pollock all over with the Lime & Ginger sauce, place into a bowl and leave for between 2–24 hours in the fridge to marinate.
2. Heat the oven to 200°C/gas mark 6.
3. Heat the red wine vinegar and sugar in a pan, pour over the onions and leave to cool.
4. Place the cabbage, radishes, avocado, onions and coriander into a bowl, mix with a drizzle of olive oil and the vinegar juice from the onions.
5. Place the pollock on a non-stick tray and cook in the oven for eight minutes.
6. Mix the Habanero sauce with the mayonnaise.
7. Season the salad with salt and pepper, lay out the tortillas, add a dollop of mayonnaise to each one, followed by some black beans and salad.
8. When the pollock is cooked, flake it into chunks and sprinkle on the tortillas. Roll them up and enjoy!

Jerk chicken wings with pineapple salsa

Recipe by Marcus Davey, Head Chef,
The Pig & Pallet, Topsham, Devon

Ingredients

10 free-range chicken wings

For the jerk wing rub

3 tbsp demerara sugar
1½ tbsp onion powder
1½ tbsp garlic powder
1 tbsp ground ginger
1 tbsp dried thyme
1 tbsp smoked paprika
1 tbsp chipotle powder
1 tbsp allspice
½ tbsp cinnamon
Salt and pepper to taste

For the pineapple salsa

1 small pineapple
1 red onion
1 lime
2 tomatoes
Bunch of chopped coriander
Bottle of Somerset Hotsauce
    Pineapple
Bottle of Somerset Hotsauce Original

Method

1 Combine all the jerk wing rub ingredients and dust the chicken wings with it. Ideally do this the day before and leave them in the fridge overnight, but if short on time, leave to marinate for at least 30 minutes.

2 Cook the chicken in one of the following ways: paint the wings with the Somerset Hot Sauce Original and cook in the oven at 180°C/gas mark 4 for 15 minutes. Using a meat probe, make sure the core temperature is over 75°C to be safe.

3 Or paint with the Original sauce and BBQ on an indirect heat (not over the coals) with a lid on until cooked to 75°C internal temperature. You can BBQ directly on the coals until cooked, but if you do, keep basting with the sauce as the wings could burn on the outside.

4 Grab a mixing bowl, and cutting into small, rough chunks, mix together the pineapple, red onion and tomatoes.

5 Add as much or as little of the Pineapple sauce as you require, think of it as a dressing, add a squeeze of lime, then sprinkle the fresh coriander and combine.

6 Serve wings on top of the salsa and enjoy!

Chef's Tip: I keep the sauce bottle handy for dipping!

ICE CREAM

Helen Taverner makes every batch of the Orange Elephant Ice Cream's award-winning products herself at her Kennford farm in Devon

We like to think the Orange Elephant is a truly 'farmhouse' ice cream. After our cows are milked in the parlour, we carry the milk across the farmyard to the barn where we make all our ice cream. I make every batch myself, so have a close eye on all stages of the process, right down to how the most important ingredient – our milk – changes through the seasons.

Coffee and chocolate are classic flavours – we've had them in the counter from day one – but, building on our experience, we wanted to see just how good our versions could become. We went back and looked closely at every element, from the custard base to the coffee and chocolate we source. After countless experiments, we came up with a high-quality twist on the old favourites. These new ones show off what we are most proud of with our ice cream – the rich creaminess that comes from the milk we look after, every step of the way, from calf to cone.

Gold and Silver winner in the Ice Cream & Sorbet category.

Orange Elephant ice cream can be purchased from the Ice Cream Parlour at Taverners Farm, Devon.

tavernersfarm.co.uk

Doughnut fritters with orange curd and chocolate ice cream

Recipe from Dasha Moughton, Head Chef,
The Vanilla Pod, Lynton, Devon

Ingredients

For the doughnut fritters
225ml water
150g butter
Pinch of salt
25g sugar
225g plain flour
4 large, free-range eggs
Vegetable oil, for frying

For the orange curd
2 large, free-range eggs, plus 2 extra
    yolks
225g caster sugar
2 large oranges, zest and juice
2 tbsp lemon juice
115g unsalted butter, cut into small
    cubes

For the cinnamon sugar
50g ground cinnamon
150g caster sugar

Four scoops of Belgian Chocolate Ice
Cream from The Orange Elephant,
Taverners Farm

Method

To make the doughnuts
1 Place the water, butter, salt and sugar into a medium-sized saucepan. Simmer the mixture for a couple of minutes until everything is dissolved and well combined.
2 Mix well and add the flour. Beat the mixture hard over the heat — when it leaves the sides of the pan it is ready. Allow it to cool completely.
3 Put the cool mixture into a food mixer, pulse briefly, then gradually add the eggs, blending as you go, to form a velvety texture.
4 Place the mixture into a piping bag. Line a tray with greaseproof paper and pipe bite-sized balls of the mix on to it.
5 Place the tray in the freezer (until the dough is solid, this will take about two to three hours).

To make the orange curd
1 Whisk the whole eggs, yolks and sugar in a heatproof bowl set over a saucepan of simmering water.
2 Whisk in the orange zest, juice and lemon juice until smooth and well combined. Continue to cook, whisking all the time, until the mixture becomes a thick, custard-like consistency.
3 Gradually add the butter, little by little, constantly whisking until the curd has emulsified.
4 Pour into a sterilised jar. Any leftover curd will keep in the fridge for about two weeks.

To fry the doughnuts
1 First, mix the cinnamon and sugar together in a bowl so it is ready for hot fritters.
2 Heat the vegetable oil in a deep-fat fryer until a piece of bread sizzles and turns golden brown. Fry the doughnuts for eight to ten minutes, or until puffed up and golden brown. You may need to cook them in batches for an even result.
3 Use a slotted spoon to carefully remove them from the hot oil, and roll the doughnuts in the cinnamon sugar.

To assemble the dish
Place a couple of spoonfuls of orange curd in the middle of a plate, put three doughnuts on top, along with a scoop of the Chocolate Ice Cream from the Orange Elephant on the side.

Chef's Tip:
If you feel like a pro chef, fill the doughnuts with the orange curd instead, by piping the curd inside!

Coffee ice cream and banana sundae with salted liqueur sauce

Ingredients

8 scoops of Coffee Ice Cream from
  The Orange Elephant, Taverners
  Farm
4 bananas
200g unsalted butter
250ml double cream, plus extra 100ml
  for whipping
350g dark muscovado sugar
1 tsp sea salt
1½ tbsp Baileys liqueur
½ tbsp Kahlúa liqueur

To decorate

Chocolate shavings
4 cocktail cherries
4 chocolate wafers
Fresh mint

Method

1 Gently melt the butter, sugar and salt together in a pan
   until the sugar dissolves.
2 Increase the heat and cook for two to three minutes.
   Keep an eye on it and stir every now and then so it
   doesn't catch on the bottom.
3 Remove from the heat, and add the cream and liqueurs.
   Be careful, as the liquid could spit and bubble.
4 Return to a gentle heat, and stir until combined and
   smooth. Set the sauce aside to cool and thicken.
5 Cut each banana in half lengthways, then cut one half into
   slices. Whip the extra cream until it turns into soft peaks.
6 Put a spoonful of the sauce in the bottom of a sundae
   glass, add the sliced banana, top with a little whipped
   cream, a little more of the sauce, then the ice cream.
7 Finally, top with a drizzle of sauce and whipped cream.
   Decorate with banana, cherry, chocolate shavings,
   chocolate wafer and mint.

Lemon posset with ice cream, summer fruits and mini meringues

Recipe by Thomas Hannon, Head Chef/Proprietor,
The Rising Sun, Truro, Cornwall

Ingredients

½ punnet of strawberries
½ punnet of raspberries
Scoop of Clotted Cream & Strawberry
    Ice Cream
Sprig of lemon balm cress

For the lemon posset

200ml lemon juice
250g caster sugar
550ml double cream

For the jelly

200ml orange juice
2 gelatine leaves, soaked in water
    until soft

For the meringues

2 egg whites
120g caster sugar

For the optional candied peel

1 orange, peel only
100ml water
100g caster sugar

Method

To make the posset

1 Reduce the lemon juice in a pan by approximately half.
2 Add the sugar, and once dissolved, add the cream.
3 Once all ingredients are incorporated, pour the mixture into four martini glasses stopping about 5ml short of the top (to leave room for the jelly topping).
4 Allow to set in the fridge for three hours.

To make the jelly topping

1 Warm up the orange juice.
2 Strain the soaked gelatine, then add to the orange juice, stirring until fully dissolved.
3 Allow to cool to room temperature, before carefully pouring on top of the possets.

To make the meringue

1 Whip the egg whites, gradually adding the sugar to form stiff peaks.
2 Using a piping bag, pipe mini meringue shapes on some parchment paper (think iced gems for size and shape).
3 Put in a warm place to dry.

To make the candied peel

1 Finely slice the orange peel.
2 Put the water and caster sugar into a pan, then bring to a simmer.
3 Add the peel and simmer for a further five minutes.
4 Remove the peel and place on baking parchment to dry for one to two hours.

To serve

5 Place some fresh strawberries, raspberries and mini meringues on top of the possets, leaving space in the middle to put a scoop of the ice cream.
6 Sprinkle the candied peel delicately on the top and add a few small lemon balm cress leaves to garnish.

Chef's Tip: If you have time to make some (or nip to the shops), a shortbread biscuit on the side is a wonderful addition.

FUDGE

Matt Jones, General Manager at Roly's Fudge Franchise, Exeter, Devon, and Matt Pugh, Franchisee at Roly's Fudge, Devon, describe the story behind two of their award-winning flavours

Matt Jones says: "Our Vanilla Clotted Cream Fudge is the traditional version of our fudge recipe, passed down by the founders of Roly's Fudge. It's been established as long as our company has – over 30 years.

"This fudge was first conjured up in the founder's 16th-century cottage, in the heart of Devon, made in antique copper pans that we still use. Real butter and milk are used – no additives, preservatives or colourings needed. The cooking process, taking over two hours per batch, means that this fudge has an indulgent creamy, yet crumbly texture. Clotted cream is swirled into it at the end of the cooking process.

"When we first entered in the Taste of the West Awards in 2009, it won Gold and has since claimed seven more. For the first time, it was a finalist in the Champion Confectionery category last year, only beaten by our own Salted Maple and Pecan Fudge!"

Matt Pugh says that the Salted Maple and Pecan Fudge was dreamt up at Roly's Fudge Pantry in Polperro. "One afternoon, we decided to push the boundaries of our already popular Cornish Sea Salt Fudge. By folding in some maple syrup and pecan nuts, it gave the fudge a whole new texture and fuller, salted caramel taste.

"The reaction from customers was amazing. It was a winning recipe and soon made in every Roly's Fudge Pantry within a few weeks. It's now one of our best-selling fudges. On its first entry to the Taste of the West Awards, it won Gold and was then announced winner of the Champion Confectionery category for 2017."

Roly's Fudge has an website so fudge fans can locate their local Roly's Fudge Pantry. They can also buy gift-wrapped boxes, delivered straight to their door.

rolysfudge.co.uk

Clotted cream fudge brownie, ice cream and summer berries

Recipe by Tom Holloway, Head Chef at the
Alexandra Hotel, Lyme Regis, Dorset

Ingredients

300g unsalted butter
125g cocoa powder
4 medium eggs
500g caster sugar
125g plain flour
150g Vanilla Clotted Cream Fudge
  from Roly's Fudge
Ice cream
Summer berries

Method

1 Preheat the oven to 170°C/gas mark 3.
2 Melt the butter with the cocoa in a microwave for about two minutes, stirring every 30 seconds until it's smooth and fully combined.
3 Using an electric mixer, whisk the eggs and sugar until pale and fluffy. Add the chocolate mix to the eggs and gently mix until fully combined.
4 Sift the flour and fold into the chocolate and egg mix.
5 Pour into a brownie tray or cake tin (buttered and lined), roughly chop up the fudge and poke into the top of the brownie mixture.
6 Place in the oven and cook for about 25–30 minutes. It should be ready when an inserted skewer comes out almost clean.
7 Serve warm with a generous scoop of vanilla ice cream and a handful of your favourite summer berries.

Vanilla clotted cream fudge and chocolate babka buns

Ingredients

For the babka buns
500g plain flour
30g caster sugar
1 tsp salt
7g dried yeast
Zest of 1 lemon
275ml full-fat milk
75g unsalted butter, room temperature
2 eggs, room temperature

For the filling
75g unsalted butter, cut into cubes
75g dark chocolate, broken into
    pieces
2 tbsp icing sugar, sifted
2 tbsp cocoa powder, sifted
75g Vanilla Clotted Cream Fudge from
    Roly's Fudge (cut into small pieces)
½ tsp sea salt flakes

For the glaze
75g caster sugar
75ml water
1 tsp vanilla extract

For the topping
75g Roly's Vanilla Clotted Cream
    Fudge (cut into pieces)

Method

To make the bun dough
1   Place the milk and butter into a small pan, and gently heat until the butter has melted. Remove from the heat and set aside to cool until it's lukewarm.
2   Put the flour, sugar and lemon zest into a large bowl. Add the salt, keeping it to one side of the bowl, then add the yeast, keeping it to the other side, to prevent them from reacting too soon.
3   Once the milk mixture is lukewarm, mix the dry ingredients together. Beat one egg in a cup with a fork and gradually add to the flour, along with the milk mixture, to form a dough (you might not need all the liquid).
4   Knead the dough for about ten minutes until smooth and elastic, then rest it in a clean, oiled bowl. Cover with cling film and allow to rise for about an hour until doubled in size.

To make the filling
1   Place the butter and chocolate into a small, heatproof bowl set over a pan of simmering water, heat until fully melted.
2   Remove from the heat and use a small whisk to mix in the icing sugar, cocoa powder and salt flakes.
3   Set aside until cooled and thickened to a spreadable consistency.

To assemble the buns
1   Lightly flour a work surface and roll the dough out into a rectangle, roughly 20cm x 30cm. Using a sharp knife or pizza cutter, cut the dough through the middle lengthwise, to make two smaller rectangle-sized pieces.

Continued on page 132...

Continued from page 130

2 Spread the chocolate filling over the dough and crumble in a little of the fudge over the top. From the long side, carefully roll up the dough to form a tight cigar shape. Do this with both rectangles.

3 Press the two ends together and twist.

4 Make a loop with the twisted dough by grabbing the two ends and crossing them over each other.

5 Push one end of the dough over the top of the dough into the hole in the middle and the other end underneath, so they both meet in the middle, forming a knot.

6 Place on to a lined baking tray, leaving at least a 5cm gap between each length, cover the tray lightly with some clingfilm, and set aside for about 45 minutes to 1 hour until risen.

7 Preheat the oven to 190°C/gas mark 5. When ready to bake, brush the buns with the remaining beaten egg. Bake for 20 minutes, or until golden brown.

To make the glaze and serve

1 Boil the sugar and water together for a couple of minutes. Remove from the heat, then add the vanilla.

2 While the buns are fresh from the oven, brush liberally with the glaze and sprinkle with a few extra pieces of chopped fudge.

3 Store in a sealed container for up to three days.

Roly's range of award-winning fudge also includes Lemon Meringue Fudge, featured in the 2017 edition of *A Taste of the West Country*

Salted Caramel & Pecan Fudge iced parfait with candied pecans

Recipe by Joe Nagy, Head Chef, The Lordleaze Hotel, Chard, Somerset

Ingredients

For the parfait

200g Salted Caramel & Pecan Fudge
    from Roly's Fudge
300ml double cream
2 large, free-range egg whites
Squeeze of lemon juice
80g caster sugar

For the pâte à bombe

100ml water
150g caster sugar
5 large free-range egg yolks

For the salted caramel sauce

200g granulated sugar
90g salted butter (at room
    temperature and cut into six)
120ml double cream
1 tsp sea salt flakes

Candied pecan nuts (for serving)

Method

To make the pâte à bombe

1 Dissolve the sugar in a medium-sized saucepan with 100ml of water. When clear, bring to the boil and place a sugar thermometer in the pan.
2 Meanwhile, whisk the egg yolks with an electric mixer until creamy. When the sugar syrup reaches 120°C, remove from the heat at once.
3 Keeping the mixer beaters running, drizzle the syrup on to the yolks and beat, on full speed, for three to five minutes, until there is a firm, yellow foam.
4 Remove and cool, whisking occasionally.

To make the parfait

1 Whisk the egg whites and lemon juice in a bowl until softly stiff, then gradually whisk in the sugar until it becomes a smooth, glossy meringue. Whip the cream in another bowl until softly stiff.
2 Fold the meringue into the pâte à bombe mix, then fold in the whipped cream.
3 Finally, crumble 200g of the fudge into the parfait mix, leaving 50g to one side to use as a garnish.
4 Spoon into eight to ten moulds and freeze until firm.

To make the sauce

1 Heat the granulated sugar in a medium saucepan over a medium heat, stirring constantly.
2 Once the sugar has dissolved, immediately add the butter.
3 Stir into the caramel for about two to three minutes, until melted.
4 Very slowly, drizzle in the cream while stirring.
5 Allow the mixture to boil for one minute. It will rise in the pan as it boils.
6 Remove from heat and stir in the salt. Allow to cool before using.

To serve, garnish with some candied pecan nuts and crumbled fudge.

Chocolate and peppermint fudge

Recipe by Emily Curry, Emily's Fudge Kitchen, Wimborne, Dorset

Ingredients

For the fudge
415g milk chocolate
105g marshmallows
105g unsalted butter
125ml whole milk
400g caster sugar
1 tsp peppermint extract

For the topping
50g white chocolate
Green food colouring

Method

To make the fudge

1 Line a 20cm x 30cm baking tray with parchment paper and set aside.
2 Make a bain-marie with a large, heatproof mixing bowl and melt the milk chocolate, then add the marshmallows. Leave to settle while you prepare the fudge base.
3 Place the sugar, butter and milk in a heavy-bottomed saucepan and stir over a medium-high heat until the sugar has dissolved. Then, bring the mixture to the boil, stirring continuously.
4 Using a sugar thermometer, measure the mixture's temperature. Keep the fudge mix at a rolling boil until it reaches 109°C – this will happen quickly. As soon as the mixture reaches temperature, remove from the heat.
5 Carefully pour the hot fudge mix over the top of the melted chocolate and marshmallows and mix until they have melted. The appearance will change from shiny to matte, and the temperature will drop. When you are at this point, beat in the peppermint extract.
6 Pour the mixture into the lined baking tray and level it off using a pallet knife or spatula.

To make the topping

1 Melt the white chocolate over a bain-marie, then mix in the green food colouring, making it as light or dark green as you like.
2 Drizzle this over the top of the tray of fudge in a design that you like (you could use a piping bag).
3 Place the tray of fudge in the fridge to allow to set for eight to ten hours, or ideally overnight. When set, cut into cubes.
4 Once cut, store the fudge in a cool place out of direct sunlight, and consume within one month.

Thank you to the following Taste of the West award-winners who made this recipe book possible

Alexandra Hotel & Restaurant
01297 442010
hotelalexandra.co.uk

Best Western Plus Centurion Hotel
01761 417711
centurionhotel.co.uk

Brian Etherington Meat Company
01209 899203
etherington-meats.co.uk

Coombe Farm Organic
01460 279509
coombefarmorganic.co.uk

Cornish Pantry, Cornwall Gold
01209 203280
cornwall-gold.com

Deli Farm Charcuterie
01840 214106
delifarmcharcuterie.co.uk

The Eastbury Hotel
01935 813131
theeastburyhotel.co.uk

Emily's Fudge Kitchen
07539 236397
emilysfudgekitchen.co.uk

Fussels Fine Foods Ltd
01373 831286
fusselsfinefoods.co.uk

Godminster
01749 813733
godminster.com

Hallett's the Bakers
01803 551901
hallettsthebakers.co.uk

The Lordleaze Hotel
01460 61066
lordleazehotel.com

LWC South West
0844 811 7399
lwc-southwest.co.uk

Mullion Cove Hotel
01326 240328
mullion-cove.co.uk

Orange Elephant Ice Cream
01392 833776
tavernersfarm.co.uk

Palmers Brewery
01308 422396
palmersbrewery.com

Roly's Fudge
01392 201059
rolysfudge.co.uk

Sea Trout Inn
01803 762274
theseatroutinn.co.uk

Sharpham Partnership Ltd
01803 732203
sharpham.com

Somerset Hotsauce Company Ltd
07554 010013
somersethotsauce.co.uk

Castle Bow Restaurant
01823 328328
castlebow.com

The Pig & Pallet
01392 668129
pigandpallet.co.uk

The Rising Sun
01872 240003
risingsuntruro.co.uk

The Vanilla Pod Restaurant
01598 753706
thevanillapodlynton.co.uk

The Three Horseshoes
01308 897259
threehorseshoes
burtonbradstock.co.uk

Treway Farm Turkeys
01726 883207
trewayfarmturkeys.co.uk

Waterside Bistro
01803 864069
watersidebistro.com

Allspice
Jerk chicken wings, pineapple salsa 116

Anchovies
Lamb chops, potatoes, salsa verde 35

Apple cider
Steak and Stilton toasted sarnie 80

Apricots
Raspberry cider and thyme sabayon 94

Asparagus
Asparagus, poached duck egg 55
Cremet and mushroom risotto 66
Cod, white wine, chive sauce 98

Avocado
Avocado, poached egg, sourdough 82
Pollock in lime & ginger sauce 115

Baileys liqueur
Coffee ice cream, banana sundae 122

Balsamic vinegar
Sausage skewers 60
Goat's cheese mousse, plums, rocket 71

Bananas
Coffee ice cream, banana sundae 122

Banana shallot
Duck, blackcurrant vodka, plum sauce 104

Barnsley lamb chops
Lamb chops, potatoes, salsa verde 35

Basil
Lamb chops, potatoes, salsa verde 35

Bay leaves
Ribeye steak, Bourguignon sauce 42
Grilled oysters, white wine sauce 100

BBQ sauce
Ribs, cider, maple glaze 92

Beef stock
Steak and Stilton toasted sarnie 80
Duck, blackcurrant vodka, plum sauce 104

Beetroots
Mackerel fillets in rapeseed oil 110

Belgian chocolate ice cream
Doughnut fritters 121

Black beans
Pollock in lime & ginger sauce 115

Blackcurrant vodka
Duck, blackcurrant vodka, plum sauce 104

Black olives
Lamb chops, potatoes, salsa verde 35

Black pepper (ground)
Ribs, cider, maple glaze 92

Breadcrumbs
Roast rack of lamb 37
Hog's Pudding Scotch eggs 58

Broccoli
Roast rack of lamb 37

Bronze Christmas Turkey
Christmas turkey salad 46
Turkey ballotine 49

Brown onion
Cheddar Dauphinoise potato gratin 74
Steak and Stilton toasted sarnie 80

Buttermilk
Rapeseed oil cake 108

Cannellini beans
Rustic salami winter stew 52

Capers
Lamb chops, potatoes, salsa verde 35

Cayenne pepper
Hog's Pudding Scotch eggs 58
Goat's cheese mousse, plums, rocket 71

CHEESE
    Blue
    Picanha steaks, blue cheese 40
    Cheese board, ice cream dessert 69

    Cheddar
    White onion, cheddar and ale soup 86

    Goat
    Roast rack of lamb 37
    Goat's cheese mousse, plums, rocket 71

Goat's cheese, rosemary cheesecake 72

Hard
Grilled oysters, white wine sauce 100

Mozzarella
Christmas turkey salad 46

Parmesan
Rustic salami winter stew 52
Cheddar Dauphinoise potato gratin 74

Sharpham Cremet
Cremet and mushroom risotto 66

Sharpham Rustic
Cheese board, ice cream dessert 69

Sharpham Ticklemore
Cheese board, ice cream dessert 69

Stilton
Steak and Stilton toasted sarnie 80

Chicken stock
Roast rack of lamb 37
Turkey ballotine 49
Rustic salami winter stew 52
White onion, cheddar and ale soup 86

Chicken wings
Jerk chicken wings, pineapple salsa 116

Chinese five-spice
Goat's cheese mousse, plums, rocket 71
Duck, blackcurrant vodka, plum sauce 104

Chipotle chilli flakes
Avocado, poached egg, sourdough 82

Chipotle powder
Ribs, cider, maple glaze 92

Chives
Hog's Pudding Scotch eggs 58
Mussels in ale 88
Cod, white wine, chive sauce 98

Chocolate shavings
Coffee ice cream, banana sundae 122

Chocolate wafers
Coffee ice cream, banana sundae 122

Cinnamon
Cheese board, ice cream dessert 69
Jerk chicken wings, pineapple salsa 116

Cinnamon (ground)
Doughnut fritters 121

Cloves
Cheese board, ice cream dessert 69

Cocktail cherries
Coffee ice cream, banana sundae 122

Cocoa powder
Clotted cream fudge brownie 128
Babka buns 130

Cod fillets
Cod, white wine, chive sauce 98

Coffee ice cream
Coffee ice cream, banana sundae 122

Conference pears
Cheese board, ice cream dessert 69

Coppa ham
Goat's cheese, rosemary cheesecake 72

Coriander
Lamb chops, potatoes, salsa verde 35
Pollock in lime & ginger sauce 115
Jerk chicken wings, pineapple salsa 116

Coriander (ground)
Ribs, cider, maple glaze 92

Corn tortillas
Pollock in lime & ginger sauce 115

Cranberries (dried)
Christmas turkey salad 46
Turkey ballotine 49

Cranberry juice
Christmas turkey salad 46

Cream cheese
Goat's cheese, rosemary cheesecake 72

Crème fraîche
White onion, cheddar and ale soup 86
Mackerel fillets in rapeseed oil 110

Cumin
Goat's cheese mousse, plums, rocket 71

Dark chocolate
Babka buns 130

Dark muscovado sugar
Coffee ice cream, banana sundae 122

Dart Valley Reserve
Cod, white wine, chive sauce 98

Dijon mustard
Lamb chops, potatoes, salsa verde 35
Christmas turkey salad 46
BBQ glazed ribs 62

Dorset Gold Ale
White onion, cheddar and ale soup 86

Dried yeast
Babka buns 130

Duck
Duck, blackcurrant vodka, plum sauce 104

Duck eggs
Asparagus, poached duck egg 55

English mustard
Hog's Pudding Scotch eggs 58

Extra virgin olive oil
Lamb chops, potatoes, salsa verde 35

Extra virgin rapeseed oil
Rapeseed oil cake 108

Fennel (ground)
Ribs, cider, maple glaze 92

Fish stock
Cod, white wine, chive sauce 98

Flank skirt steak
Steak and Stilton toasted sarnie 80

French mustard
Hog's Pudding Scotch eggs 58

Garlic
Lamb chops, potatoes, salsa verde 35
Roast rack of lamb 37
Ribeye steak, Bourguignon sauce 42
Rustic salami winter stew 52
Sausage skewers 60
Cremet and mushroom risotto 66
Goat's cheese mousse, plums, rocket 71
Cheddar Dauphinoise potato gratin 74
Steak and Stilton toasted sarnie 80
Mussels in ale 88

Garlic powder
Ribs, cider, maple glaze 92
Jerk chicken wings, pineapple salsa 116

Garlic salami

Asparagus, poached duck egg 55

Gelatine leaves
Cheese board, ice cream dessert 69
Lemon posset 125

Ginger
Goat's cheese mousse, plums, rocket 71

Ginger (ground)
Jerk chicken wings, pineapple salsa 116

Habanero sauce
Pollock in lime & ginger sauce 115

Hazelnuts
Goat's cheese mousse, plums, rocket 71
Goat's cheese, rosemary cheesecake 72

Hog's Pudding
Hog's Pudding Scotch eggs 58

Honey
Goat's cheese, rosemary cheesecake 72

Honeycomb
Goat's cheese, rosemary cheesecake 72

Honey (runny)
Sausage skewers 60

Horseradish
Mackerel fillets in rapeseed oil 110

Hot peppery salami
Rustic salami winter stew 52

Ice cream
Lemon posset 125
Clotted cream fudge brownie 128

Juniper (ground)
Ribs, cider, maple glaze 92

Kahlúa liqueur
Coffee ice cream, banana sundae 122

Lamb
Roast rack of lamb 37

Leaven
Sourdough bread 78

Leeks
Rustic salami winter stew 52

Lemon
Asparagus, poached duck egg 55

Cheese board, ice cream dessert 69
Mackerel fillets in rapeseed oil 110
Doughnut fritters 121
Lemon posset 125
Babka buns 130

Lemon balm cress
Lemon posset 125

Lime
Avocado, poached egg, sourdough 82
Jerk chicken wings, pineapple salsa 116

Lime & ginger sauce
Pollock in lime & ginger sauce 115

Mackerel fillets
Mackerel fillets in rapeseed oil 110

Maple syrup
Ribs, cider, maple glaze 92

Marshmallows
Chocolate, peppermint fudge 136

Mayonnaise
Hog's Pudding Scotch eggs 58
Pollock in lime & ginger sauce 115

Milk chocolate
Chocolate, peppermint fudge 136

Mint
Lamb chops, potatoes, salsa verde 35
Coffee ice cream, banana sundae 122

Modern Craft Cider
Ribs, cider, maple glaze 92

Multi-seed loaf
Steak and Stilton toasted sarnie 80

Mushrooms (chestnut)
Ribeye steak, Bourguignon sauce 42
Cremet and mushroom risotto 66

Mussels
Mussels in ale 88

Mustard powder
Ribs, cider, maple glaze 92

Nutmeg
Cheddar Dauphinoise potato gratin 74

Onion
Turkey ballotine 49
Cremet and mushroom risotto 66

Onion powder
Ribs, cider, maple glaze 92
Jerk chicken wings, pineapple salsa 116

Orange
Doughnut fritters 121
Lemon posset 125

Orange juice
Lemon posset 125

Pancetta
Ribeye steak, Bourguignon sauce 42

Panko breadcrumbs
Cheddar Dauphinoise potato gratin 74

Parsley
Lamb chops, potatoes, salsa verde 35
BBQ glazed ribs 62
Cremet and mushroom risotto 66
Mussels in ale 88

Pasteurised egg
Cheese board, ice cream dessert 69

Peaches
Raspberry cider and thyme sabayon 94

Peas
Cremet and mushroom risotto 66

Pecan nuts (candied)
Fudge iced parfait 135

Peppermint extract
Chocolate, peppermint fudge 136

Picanha steaks
Picanha steaks, blue cheese 40

Pineapple
Jerk chicken wings, pineapple salsa 116

Pistachio
Raspberry cider and thyme sabayon 94

Pork belly ribs
Ribs, cider, maple glaze 92

Plums
Goat's cheese mousse, plums, rocket 71
Duck, blackcurrant vodka, plum sauce 104

Pollock fillet
Pollock in lime & ginger sauce 115

Pork ribs

BBQ glazed ribs 62

Potatoes
Lamb chops, potatoes, salsa verde 35
Roast rack of lamb 37
Picanha steaks, blue cheese 40
Ribeye steak, Bourguignon sauce 42
Turkey ballotine 49
Cheddar Dauphinoise potato gratin 74
Cod, white wine, chive sauce 98

Potato (mashed)
BBQ glazed ribs 62

Rack of lamb
Roast rack of lamb 37

Radishes
Pollock in lime & ginger sauce 115

Rainbow chard
Cremet and mushroom risotto 66

Raspberries
Lemon posset 125

Raspberry cider
Raspberry cider and thyme sabayon 94

Red onion
Lamb chops, potatoes, salsa verde 35
Sausage skewers 60
Pollock in lime & ginger sauce 115
Jerk chicken wings, pineapple salsa 116

Red rice
Rustic salami winter stew 52

Red spring onions
Cod, white wine, chive sauce 98

Red wine
Roast rack of lamb 37
Ribeye steak, Bourguignon sauce 42
Turkey ballotine 49
Rustic salami winter stew 52
Cheese board, ice cream dessert 69

Red wine vinegar
Lamb chops, potatoes, salsa verde 35
Pollock in lime & ginger sauce 115

Ribeye steaks
Ribeye steak, Bourguignon sauce 42

Risotto rice
Cremet and mushroom risotto 66

Rocket
Christmas turkey salad 46
Goat's cheese mousse, plums, rocket 71

Rock oysters
Grilled oysters, white wine sauce 100

Vanilla Clotted Cream Fudge
Babka buns 130

Rosemary
Roast rack of lamb 37
Sausage skewers 60
Goat's cheese, rosemary cheesecake 72
Rapeseed oil cake 108

Rosemary water biscuits
Goat's cheese mousse, plums, rocket 71
Goat's cheese, rosemary cheesecake 72

Rum
Cheese board, ice cream dessert 69

Salami
Rustic salami winter stew 52

Salted Caramel & Pecan Fudge
Fudge iced parfait 135

Samphire
Cod, white wine, chive sauce 98

Sausage meat
Turkey ballotine 49
Hog's Pudding Scotch eggs 58

Sea salt flakes
Babka buns 130
Fudge iced parfait 135

Serrano ham
Christmas turkey salad 46
Turkey ballotine 49

Sesame seeds
Sausage skewers 60

Shallots
Ribeye steak, Bourguignon sauce 42
Rustic salami winter stew 52
Mussels in ale 88
Grilled oysters, white wine sauce 100

Sharpham Sparkling Blanc
Grilled oysters, white wine sauce 100

Smoked paprika
Ribs, cider, maple glaze 92

Jerk chicken wings, pineapple salsa 116

Smoked rapeseed oil
Mackerel fillets in rapeseed oil 110

Smoked streaky bacon
Ribeye steak, Bourguignon sauce 42

Somerset Hotsauce Original
Jerk chicken wings, pineapple salsa 116

Somerset Hotsauce Pineapple
Jerk chicken wings, pineapple salsa 116

Star anise
Turkey ballotine 49
Goat's cheese mousse, plums, rocket 71
Duck, blackcurrant vodka, plum sauce 104

Strawberries
Lemon posset 125

Sugar snap peas
Cremet and mushroom risotto 66

Summer berries
Clotted cream fudge brownie 128

Tally ho! Ale
Mussels in ale 88

Tenderstem broccoli
Turkey ballotine 49

Thyme
Ribeye steak, Bourguignon sauce 42
Hog's Pudding Scotch eggs 58
Cheddar Dauphinoise potato gratin 74
Steak and Stilton toasted sarnie 80
White onion, cheddar and ale soup 86
Raspberry cider and thyme sabayon 94

Thyme (dried)
Jerk chicken wings, pineapple salsa 116

Tomatoes
Lamb chops, potatoes, salsa verde 35
Sausage skewers 60
BBQ glazed ribs 62
Jerk chicken wings, pineapple salsa 116

Tomatoes (chopped)
Rustic salami winter stew 52

Tomatoes (piccolo)
Rustic salami winter stew 52

Tomato purée

Ribeye steak, Bourguignon sauce 42

Vanilla clotted cream fudge
Clotted cream fudge brownie 128
Babka buns 130

Vanilla extract
Babka buns 130

Vanilla pod
Cheese board, ice cream dessert 69

Vegetable stock
Roast rack of lamb 37
Cremet and mushroom risotto 66

Walnuts
Cheese board, ice cream dessert 69

Watercress
BBQ glazed ribs 62
Mackerel fillets in rapeseed oil 110

Wheal Rose glazed pork ribs
BBQ glazed ribs 62

Wheal Rose pork sausage
Sausage skewers 60

White cabbage
Pollock in lime & ginger sauce 115

White chocolate
Chocolate, peppermint fudge 136

White onions
White onion, cheddar and ale soup 86

White wine
Asparagus, poached duck egg 55
Cremet and mushroom risotto 66

White wine vinegar
Asparagus, poached duck egg 55
BBQ glazed ribs 62
Steak and Stilton toasted sarnie 80

Wholegrain mustard
Ribeye steak, Bourguignon sauce 42

Yeast
Sourdough bread 78

Yellow bell pepper
Sausage skewers 60